When Spirits Speak: A Gathering of Heroes

Stories of U.S. Soldiers in Vietnam

Jeri K. Tory Conklin

BALBOA PRESS
A DIVISION OF HAY HOUSE

ISBN: 9781452560816 (sc)
ISBN: 9781452560809 (e)

Library of Congress Control Number: 2012920013

Balboa Press books may be ordered through booksellers or by contacting:
Balboa Press
A Division of Hay House
1663 Liberty Drive
Bloomington, IN 47403
www.balboapress.com
1-(877) 407-4847

Illustration© "Last Letter Home" by Teri Ann "Sunny" Henderson, 2012
Cover photograph© (1961) used with permission of the Tory family.
Cover designed by Jeri K. Tory Conklin
Foreword © Bill Bonnichsen, 2012

Printed in the United States of America

Balboa Press rev. date: 10/18/2012

Also by author:

When Spirits Speak: Messages from Spirit Children

Dedicated to all servicemen and women
who have fought for this great country of ours
and who have mailed their last letters home.
Some have gone on to the world of spirit; the rest
walk amongst us and remind us
of our own patriotic duty
in whatever military actions come our way.

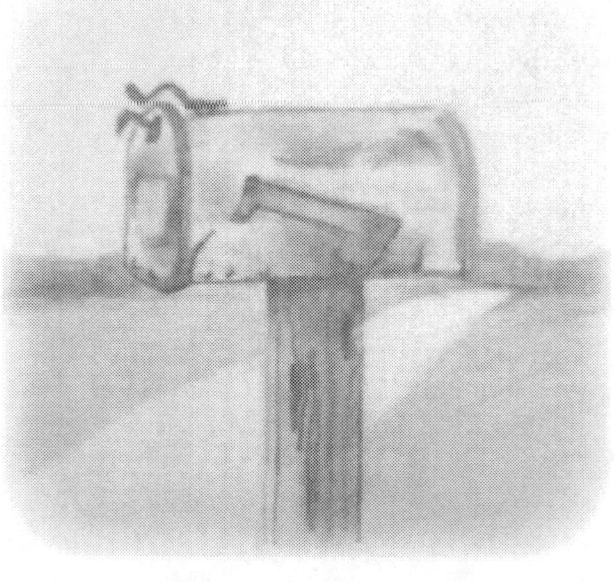

Teri Ann "Sunny" Henderson, 2012

"Last Letter Home"

Contents

Foreword

I've been married for almost thirty years. My wife has asked me many times why I won't talk about Vietnam. The easy answer would be to say that it just brings back too many painful memories and nightmares of war, killing and dying. The real answer is that unless you were there and felt the emotions that come from seeing close friends die so violently, then you won't understand or feel what so many returning Marines, soldiers and sailors felt, so trying to explain has always felt like such a futile task.

Two thoughts come to mind as I read Jeri's manuscript. First, as a nineteen year old Marine when I arrived in Vietnam in June of 1966 I believed I was invincible and would make it home in good shape. Death would happen to the "other guy", not me. I'm sure every person had the same feeling. I did make it back home and didn't think too much of how dangerous it was. Forty six years later I think back to some of the operations I was involved in and it scares me. I could have died! I wasn't invincible, just young, naïve and lucky. My second and much more emotional thought is for all the young men who were carried off the field of battle by the "White Soldier" at such an early age. I went back home after thirteen months and led a life as all young men and women should. I partied, dated women, got an entry level job that supported me and held a bright future. I met that special lady and got married, had a beautiful family and retired after forty years at the same job.

The young men who Jeri spoke to never had that chance. Although the taking of young, innocent lives is in the forefront of the minds of war proponents and pacifists alike, the grim reality of the lives lost is something I have never been able to justify in my mind. It has never been right and never will be.

Jeri Tory Conklin's book, When Spirits Speak: A Gathering of Heroes is a fascinating read for people of all ages and beliefs. Through another dimension, Jeri has chosen to enlighten us and share her conversations and interviews with fine young men who gave their all for their country.

Please take time to read Jeri's book, think about the men brought to her, reflect on the meaning of each individual story and feel comfortable knowing these young men who paid the ultimate sacrifice are finally getting the chance to tell their stories.

-Bill Bonnichsen, U.S. Marine Corps 1965-1968

Preface

Communicating With the World of Spirit

All beings, whether seen or unseen,
have the ability to communicate with
and understand each other.

I have been communicating with the world of spirit since I was born. I never questioned my ability to speak with or see spirits, those children, adults, or animals whose life energy had left their bodies and moved to the nonphysical plane, or "the other side." I just didn't understand why adults didn't see or hear them. Then, when I was ten, my father was killed, and I shut down my communication with the world of spirit.

In 1994, as an adult, I began to allow spirit communication back into my life when I connected with two earthbound spirit children at my home in Idaho. But it wasn't until one day in 2007, as I sat on a beach in Cape Cod, counting the waves and seeking change and healing, that I realized communicating with the world of spirit and sharing those messages with others must be a way back to living the life I was meant to live. So I listened.

Each and every one of us, not just me, came into this lifetime knowing that we could communicate with the world of spirit. When we are young children, the veil between the spirit home we have just left and our new, earthly home is thin. Not only do we communicate with those spirits we've left behind, but our soul also moves freely between the two dimensions. If we are born into a family that accepts our ability to communicate telepathically with spirits, then we are encouraged and supported. If not, then we bow to social and parental pressures, wrapping our knowledge in oilskin and tucking it away in our secret box where it will be safe until we can use it again.

The means by which I communicate with spirits probably most resembles what we think of as telepathy, or the exchange of information through thought. Telepathic communication has been going on in various cultures since the beginning of time as we know it. Considered a universal ability, telepathy is shared by all as inhabitants of Mother Earth. Before there was a vocal spoken language, telepathic communication—or "mind talk," as I call it—was all there was.

I communicate with the world of spirit using the three most common forms of spiritual communication:

> **Clairvoyance (visual communication),** which allows us to see others' thoughts or information not necessarily with our physical eyes, but rather as colors, forms, and textures in our mind's eye (also known as the third eye). For example, I see entities or spirits as if they were fully embodied people standing right in front of me.

> **Clairaudience (auditory communication),** which allows us to hear others' thoughts or receive information not with our physical ears, but as voices in our minds. When I speak with spirits, I hear what they are saying as clearly as I hear people in ordinary reality speaking. The voices of the spirits I hear sound just like those of people I speak with in regular conversations, but I hear their voices within my head.

> **Clairsentience (tactile communication),** in which we pick up thoughts and information and convert them into a feeling, be it emotional or physical. You may feel the information as calming feelings, as a prickly sensation, or as the hairs on your arms and back of your neck standing up. As you begin to differentiate types of spiritual energies, you will come to recognize the different feelings or sensations each triggers for you. For example, when I am in the presence

> of a spiritual entity, my legs begin to tingle. I can also tell whether an entity has actually left a physical body and is now on the other side, or is still inhabiting a body on the physical plane and using the world of spirit as a means to communicate with me, by how heavy or dense its energy feels.

The spirits that “come through” the spiritual world to me may be those who have left their physical bodies and now are back home in the world of spirit, or they may still be inhabiting physical bodies here on earth, but have left their bodies temporarily to meet me on the nonphysical, spiritual plane.

When I telepathically talk with the spirits that come to me, I can only describe my consciousness as a deep meditative state. While my physical body remains in the chair on the physical plane, my soul is in the nonphysical realm, acting as an observer and participant on the nonphysical plane. There I am able to interact with spirits as if we both were still in physical bodies. I see/visualize each spirit as an image with a face and a body. I see their essence, their aura (energy field). Linear time passes while I am away from the physical, though I am unaware of its passing. Depending upon how much time I have spent away from my physical body, it can take some time for me to readjust to it when I return.

Communication with the world of spirit can be done any time, any place. It doesn’t require anything other than for you to show up and ask questions with respect and appreciation. Communicating with spiritual beings—whether they are angels and fairies, the spirits of children or soldiers who have died, or the spirits of animals, rocks or trees—is as simple as sitting quietly and allowing yourself to hear or see what they would have you know. Their voices are, quite simply the still, small voice you hear in your head, see in your mind's eye, or feel with your body or emotions.

My work with the world of spirit is inspired by a higher power, which I know as "God." Bringing forth spirit stories in a published format is my way of saying, "I am a communicator with the world of spirit. This is who I am, and what I do." As our soul moves into greater spiritual evolution, I believe it is important to see more accounts of communication with the world of spirit in written form, so that others might realize this communication is possible.

I believe that God speaks to and through each of us in many different ways—including through the voices of those in the world of spirit—in an attempt to remind us of the home we left behind when our souls chose to incarnate into physical bodies. This book of stories from hero soldiers, will, I hope, inspire *faith,* by showing there is a God in heaven, waiting for us to return; *hope,* by showing there is life after the passing of the physical body; and the knowledge that *love* knows no bounds, as our loved ones come back to tell us they are safe and with us still in spirit, if not in body. If you have lost a loved one, or if one of the soldiers included in this book is related to you, please know they are safe and with God.

It is not always easy or even possible to document and validate the authenticity of the information provided by those speaking from the world of spirit. Growing in trust and faith in the unseen world is, however, a rewarding experience. With each communication I receive from those who have passed and are in the world of spirit, my faith grows in my ability to bring forth the gifts they entrust to me.

Introduction

In the summer of 2007, as I sat on the beach at Cape Cod, a group of spirit children appeared to me and asked me to write down stories of their lives and their passing, as well as their messages for their parents. Their words would become the basis for my first book, *When Spirits Speak: Messages from Spirit Children* (2011).

As my conversations with the spirit children came to a close early in 2011, I asked them to gather together one more time for a Question and Answer session to end the book. Suddenly, a hush fell over them, and a pathway opened in their midst. A combat-weary, bloodied soldier moved forward, supported by one child after the other, until he stood before me. I knew instinctively that he was appearing in this guise to make clear to me the way he had passed.

"Writer, you aren't finished yet. Will you write our story?" he asked, his voice pleading. Kneeling down on one knee, he unshouldered his M-16 rifle and leaned on it for support. He said to me:

This is your next book, Writer. The children saw me coming and stepped aside. Not in fear, though I am pretty ragged looking after all those months in the jungle. No, they knew. They knew I had to come through now to prepare you for what lies ahead.

So much blood has been shed; so many boys and men have lost their lives. Writer, please listen as we tell our stories of our last hours on the earth plane. None of us were alone when we passed; the White Soldier[1] was with each of us to bring us home. We are at peace now. We want our families to understand and be at peace as well. Are you ready, Writer? My men are right here, so eager for you to do this for us.

So I began writing down the stories told to me by the soldiers who passed through the sea of children that day. All of the soldiers who spoke with me had fought and passed in Vietnam between 1965 and 1975.

The stories in this book are from soldiers who have passed and soldiers who were living at the time they first contacted me via the world of spirit, but who have since passed. Their stories are filled with the dreams of young men who grew into adults all too quickly in a land not their own. They speak of the bond between soldiers, the brotherhood that stands the test of time and distance; the fear they lived with each day; how they wrote letters that

1 The White Soldier is described in detail in chapter 2.

would be sent to their families if they were killed; and the simple things they came to take for granted. Some speak of their love of Vietnam and its people. And many of them convey their last few hours on the earth plane.[2]

One of the things I hope you take away from these soldiers' messages and stories is the knowledge that there a place beyond our earthly home, a place waiting patiently for our spirits' return to the nonphysical. The soldiers have come through to reassure us that *no one* passes alone, not even a soldier on a field of battle. God always comes Himself and/or sends angels. For soldiers, He comes appearing as "the White Soldier." As you'll read in chapter 3, each of the men who shared the experience of their passing with me spoke of this White Soldier. In chapter 2, I share my own encounter with the White Soldier, plus a story of a friend's father who saw Him on the battlefield as well.

The stories in this book are also but a small reminder of the sacrifice our military men and women endure each and every day for our freedom as a country and individually. If you were one of those who didn't welcome our soldiers home from

---

2 Time does not exist in the world of spirit. So when the men were telling their stories, they were simultaneously showing the events to me as they were living and remembering those same events happening in the past. This is why they speak in both the present and past tense when talking with me, as you'll notice when reading their accounts in chapter 3.

Vietnam at the time, perhaps now, your eyes will be opened as to what they experienced. Perhaps you can find a new understanding through which to know their sacrifices. It is never too late to say, "Thank you for your service" to any active duty soldier, veteran, or family member of a fallen soldier who gave his or her life for country.

The American soldiers sought me out to write this book; I am "the Writer," and these are their stories. If these tales from veterans bring about a healing of spirit, then my ultimate wish is fulfilled.

So it is I bring to you small snippets of the Vietnam War as seen from the "other side."

1

Coming to Vietnam

I remember: The children would come up tugging on our clothes, bedraggled, starving, and we had to throw away food because our government said, "Throw food over board before coming into port."
Bob, Saigon, 1966

TIMOTHY

Timothy is a self-described Iowa farm boy who at the time of this writing had not passed. He appeared to me as a spirit, though I knew by the feel of his energy that his spirit was still in the physical world. Its energy was heavier than that of a spirit who had passed. Timothy used what I term "telepathy" to speak to me while he was still in physical. He wanted to share his love of Vietnam, the land he served in as a U.S. soldier and came to love as much as the farm of his childhood.

Once upon a time, in the land of dragons and fairies, into the verdant green jungles of a place far from home, a soldier came—many soldiers. Young men, some still considered young boys by their mothers, were dropped through the jungle canopy to emerge in a war zone below. The canopy of green was deceiving. From ten thousand feet in the air, it resembled heads of broccoli. It was lighter in color perhaps, but still, crowns of the trees bunched together. Underneath the canopy were jungles of death and destruction. I was but one of those young men, just eighteen at the time I was drafted.

Coming from my own country, which had not seen war on her soil for over 100 years, I didn't know this new land had once been at peace, run by the yin and yang of nature's own clock.[3] The ebb and flow of the tides, and time and energy, worked in concert with each other. The peacefulness of this pastoral landscape would not last long, as communism was soon to invade the northern part of the land to begin its push into southern Vietnam. When America entered the war, the other intruder into this once peaceful setting was the soldier. Soldiers from many

---

3 Refers to the interconnectedness and interdependence on the natural world. The shadow and light; male and female energies.

nations had come to take their turn in the Vietnam jungles, until it was finally America's turn.

Home bred and corn fed, I had an innocence like that of a small stone cast upon the waters of a pond. Ripples at the point of its entrance spread out in all directions, eventually reaching the shore. Little did I know that one day my presence in a land far away, a land where I had been sent to kill the dragons, would eventually kill me—not because of a bullet, but because of my love for a country and its people that were not my own.

It is true—I am just an Iowa farm boy, born and bred. The dust of the fields runs through my veins. My body feels the drought as much as it feels the rain. I learned to hunt and kill as a means of providing food for the table, never for sport. There is no sport in killing a beautiful animal. It was always my job to kill the chickens and pigs, sheep and calves as I grew older. If there was one thing about the farm I abhorred, it was that killing was required. I taught myself to do it as painlessly as possible, for it hurt me as much, if not more, than it did them. I wanted to work with the soil, not kill.

Drafted the fall of 1966, just out of high school the summer before, I hadn't had time to even get in trouble yet. Not that I would have; I was a pretty straight kid. My pop depended on me to help with all the farmin' and chores, so it left little time for getting in trouble. Sunup to sundown, we worked on the farm, day in and day out.

Most of my friends hated the farm, couldn't wait to get away from it. Hated the hard work, hated how tied down they were. Going to college wasn't an option for most of us. Farming doesn't bring in a lot of extra money, usually just enough to get by and cover the expenses for planting the next year. Joining the army wasn't the best way to get off the farm, but it was one way—an honorable way at least. Little did any of us know that the day we left the farm and the dust on our shoes behind, we would never see it again.

I was just a farm boy with no idea what to expect in the coming months or years. For the time being, I just wanted to get through basic training, as we were being herded around like a bunch of sheep. I realized what it must have been like for farm animals. All they wanted was to do their work, eat, and sleep. That is all I wanted to do. Sleep escaped us, day in and day out, but work and eating never did. Food wasn't too bad—wasn't too good, either. There wasn't a day or two that went by that I was wishing for a plate of Mom's Sunday fried chicken and mashed potatoes, the white ones. The potatoes there were tinged green.

Basic Training changed for the better once we were issued our weapon, an M-16 rifle; it became our closest companion day and night. I had to change my perception of a gun and its usefulness. Now it became a weapon to save my life by taking a life. It was drilled into us to learn her inside and out. Ole' Bess I called her, after Daniel Boone's rifle. Me and Bess. I learned every inch of her, just as instructed. I listened to her. The guys thought I was crazy. Maybe I was. But on some days after cleaning her, I could hear her whisper, "Thank you." I didn't go anywhere without Bess, and in the coming days and months, she was to become my closest friend.

I landed in the hot, steamy jungles of Vietnam on Thanksgiving Day, 1966. I would have much preferred to be home on the farm, where I knew there would be a tom turkey on the table with all the fixins. I wonder who killed the turkey this year. Perhaps my brother had taken over my job; he was awful young, though.

"Killin' makes you a man," my pop used to say. I didn't see it that way, not even now. Killing to eat and killing to survive are two vastly different events.

And so it was that I found myself out on patrol that first night after arrival at camp. "Perimeter duty" they called it. Walkin' the wire. Shoot to kill anything that moves—those were my orders. I was grateful for the sun coming up that next morning, as it meant my duty was over and I could finally sleep.

Sleep in a combat zone is not the same sleep as back home on the farm, in my nice warm bed, where

Grandma's handmade quilt kept me warm. No, sleep in the combat zone was with one ear and one eye open at all times. It was a restless sleep where every single noise jolts you awake. Bess slept with me, even during the day, my finger always on the trigger just in case.

There were farms all around our base camp. Everywhere you looked the open land was planted in rice. I found it strange that while the farmers had oxen, most of the time, the women were out in the fields with sticks, poking holes in the ground to plant the seeds. The oxen were used more for the harvest than the planting. I eventually learned that the Montagnard (the Vietnamese mountain people, whom the Vietnamese creation myth says are descendants of a fairy queen and her fifty sons) did not believe in plowing up the soil, for it disturbed the spirits of the earth.

Normally we wouldn't be in one place too long, but for a month we stayed and fought the war from our base camp. This staying put gave me an opportunity to meet some of the local farmers. Who would have thought that I, an Iowa farm boy, would be sitting there talking with a Vietnamese farmer about farming? While our crops were totally different—his rice, mine corn and wheat—we actually shared the same love of the land upon which we farmed. [We shared] a common bond, away from the war—true farmers at heart.

I told him of my tractor and how much easier it was to plow the land. He told me how he has farmed the same way as his father and his father before him. Out of respect for the land, they did little to disturb its spirit. He told me that my tractor "must create great noise so the Spirit cannot hear herself sing." Perhaps this was true. Farming in America had come a long way since the day of using a hand plow to plant and till the soil.

Much like in our own farming families, every member of the [Vietnamese farming] household joined in with daily work in the field. There was nothing mechanized in the farming process there. Everything was done by hand—sowing, reaping, drying of the rice before it was sacked and taken into the market. It was all done by hand. And yet they were not behind us because they farmed in what we would consider the "old fashion way." No, they were following the ways of their ancestors, honoring the spirit of land so they could hear her sing her songs of gratitude.

I know Pop wouldn't consider giving up his tractor. [*Here, Timothy laughed, and I saw his face was relaxed.*] But I thought maybe we could try hand-plowing a small plot for the vegetable garden when I get back home.

With farming there is always much to talk about—the weather, the prices at the grange for our crops. Never would we talk about war back home. But in Vietnam, war was all there was to talk about. When in camp or on patrol, we lived, breathed, and ate war and all its many tentacles. I lived to talk farming with my new family and forget about the war for a few moments each day, even when that war was on their land and I was the intruder.

Today, the smell of rain permeates the jungle. It is not the smell of fresh, clean rain like I have in Iowa. Rather, it's the smell of a hot, sultry rain. It is heavy in its presence and carries with it the blood of war. There is nothing for it to wash clean here. Blood is everywhere. It runs in the streams; it runs across the land. The jungle undergrowth is massive in appearance, fed by the blood of soldiers from both countries. Attempts to chop through its dense growth are met with resistance. Perhaps indicative of the strong will of its people, neither the land nor its undergrowth readily yields to the machete blade.

I live in a state of wetness. Nothing I wear is ever dry. If it isn't the rain, it is the sweat of the jungle heat. I dream of one day being dry again. I try hard to imagine how that dryness would actually feel. My hands and feet swell with the wetness, then shrivel up when they are oversaturated.

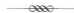

In the beginning, I welcomed the daily rains, allowing them to wash away the filth of war. I am just a simple farm boy from Iowa; I'm not a killer. Now, after all these months, the rains just bring more blood. Will the day come when there is no longer any blood to wash away? Is that even possible?

They are starting again. Like clockwork, on the dot, without fail, every day for the next six months. Funny how the rains are the only constant I have to look forward to each day. I know the rains will come. I can count on them. They never disappoint me.

One month after being in-country, our platoon began the move north. Vietnam is such a beautiful country, even with all the war and killing that went on. Her people just took everything in stride. They knew the spirits of the land would walk with them through the dark hours, during the heaviest storms, and still bring them out into the light when it was over. They didn't miss a step; they just kept marching forward. When a volley of artillery or a firefight lasting long into the night pushing them back, they got up the next morning, gave honor to the spirits of the new day, and just moved forward.

Rather than mourn the loss of possessions, they gave thanks for what was left. They grieved for the loss of their family, but knew their souls had just moved to another field and would be there, watching over them. Even in death, the Vietnamese honor the spirits of their fallen family members on a daily basis. The yin and yang in action. They are not gone; they are just not "here."

Of the many memories I will cherish of this time in Vietnam, that is the phrase I will remember always: “They are not gone. They just are not here.” On days when I get to missing the farm, my family, my friends, I tell myself, “They are not gone. They are just not here.”

Mya and Staff Sergeant Joe

When I began writing the soldiers' stories, Staff Sergeant Joe first came through to me in spirit not to tell of his passing, but to speak of helping a Vietnamese family and their child, whom he called Mya. I met with Staff Sergeant Joe two more times before finishing his story. At the time I first met with him, he had not passed, but before I'd finished getting down his story, he had.

As Joe began talking to me, I also felt the presence of a female energy wanting to come through. Because of its heaviness, I knew this spirit, like Joe's and Timothy's, had yet not passed from the physical. I was able to perceive this energy as female because it looked like a woman when I saw it.

That energy belonged to Mya, a Vietnamese woman who, as a young girl, was caught in the war on her land. She shared her own side of Staff Sergeant Joe's story—the story of the kind American GI who helped her and her family. Together, their accounts form the story of an unlikely friendship between a child and a soldier during a time of war.

I am grateful to Joe and Mya for both giving me their stories via telepathy.

Mya: My name is Mya. I knew one of your American GIs. He was so kind to me and my family.

My father, he worked hard in the fields only to have the napalm bombs destroy our crops. If we didn't farm, we didn't eat. Many nights we went hungry since the war began. Mother, she cried because she could not feed us. There was nothing, not even a little rice.

Your GI, he brought us food—food in cans. We boiled water and put it in the can and it mades food! You are very smart peoples to learn to make food in a can.[4] It [was] good food.

Joe: Yes, I fed her family while we were in the area, fighting. So much destruction, some of it so unnecessary. Charlie[5] was everywhere, attacking us during the day and then disappearing into the villages at night. We just destroyed everything in our efforts to rout him out. He was the enemy we couldn't see. Wipe out everything around us, and perhaps we would find him. While we may have been the hand that pulled the trigger, Charlie's appearance was the cause and his disappearance was the effect. He was an invisible enemy of sorts. The strategy, therefore,

---

4 Mya is referring to the C rations the GIs carried with them on patrols. There would be a can containing rice or some other dehydrated type of meal to which you added boiling water. Then there were cans containing a dessert, as well as a packet of instant coffee, a package of crackers, a piece of candy, and a small can opener called a P-38.

5 *Charlie* was common GI slang for the Viet Cong and its soldiers.

was to just take out anything and everything he could hide within.

For many of these people—Mya's people, for instance—there was a war going on, but it wasn't with them. They just wanted to be left alone to farm and eke out a living on their land. That was their life, not this war. Even in the midst of battle, we would see them out tilling the earth. I was amazed that life somehow managed to grow in the midst of such destruction. You know, Writer, it was our war, not theirs. All they wanted to do was farm and live out their lives in the way of their ancestors. RPGs [rocket propelled grenades] would be falling from the sky, and yet they were out in their fields, plowing, planting, and harvesting the rice that would feed them until the next crop. What Charlie did was Charlie's business; what they did was farm—or at least try to.

Mya: Your GI, he was tall and skinny. He had to bend down to get in our hut. We very short peoples. He didn't fit our house. So many nights we [were] without food until the bombing moved on. Father and your GI talked for hours and spent much time laughing. I think neither knew what the other was saying, but the language of love is universal, is it not? Everyone can feel love.

We were grateful to your American GI, for he shared with us his meals. We were sad to see him go, but he had to follow the war as it moved on.

It was good to know that there would be another Vietnamese family who would get to meet your American GI and share his food in a box with him. I, myself, missed him greatly, for he was kind to me. He taught me words in English: "Good morning. How are you? My name is Mya. What is yours?" Not too bad is it, Writer?

Joe: This is how I met Mya. She was a young child then, maybe four or five years old. She was scrawny and barefoot, holding onto her mama's skirt as her mama worked the fields alongside her father. I had watched them for several days, intrigued and mystified at their continued farming. Bombs and bullets falling all around—you should be scared and running for cover. Not these people. The daily routines of their life continued in the midst of all the killing. How does one do that, Writer—go about their daily routines in the field, while death is falling all around them? Perhaps the will to live, the will to survive, is stronger than the fear of death itself. Perhaps if there is a peaceful understanding about death, then there is no fear of dying. Dying is just another of those routine tasks performed each day. If it is your day to go, then the angel of death will find you toiling away in the fields and just pluck you from behind the oxen. Life will not stop because you have died.

We saw death often amongst the villagers and farmers, victims caught in the cross fire between us and the North Vietnamese. They would fall out of line, and someone else would move up to take their place. Their bodies were left in the fields until the end of the day, when family members would go retrieve them for honoring and burial.

The villagers knew that anything that moved at night was suspected of being Charlie and would be killed Yet they went on with their lives and routine as if we weren't even there and there wasn't a war raging all around them.

The day I met Mya's family, the farmers had been working the fields. One by one, families had begun to disappear. It was as if the earth just swallowed them up. Our months of surveillance had taught us to beware when bodies disappeared in the field. It was as if a silent call went out for everyone to get out of the way, for Charlie was coming.

And so it happened that day. Bodies behind Mya's family began to disappear, and soon they were all that was left standing in the field. I made my way over to them, using whatever shrubbery I could find as cover. Mya's father raised his arms in surrender when I emerged from the brush. I shook my head and turned him around to see that there was no one behind him. Intent on plowing his field, he had failed to see the disappearances. A look of terror crossed his face, and he quickly gathered his wife and daughter and left the field, leaving the family ox to make its way home.

Within minutes, the green field erupted with gunfire and black-pajama-clad bodies. Out of the rice stocks they arose. I found myself a sitting duck and quickly made my way back to my patrol, grateful for the darkness falling around me. I would later hear about leaving my patrol, but right now it was just about the fire fight ahead.

Just as quietly as they had arisen from the rice paddies, so too did they disappear—perfectly orchestrated as if by some puppet master in the sky, pulling strings. Now you see them, now you don't. We returned to base camp just as the orange streaks of morning broke the darkened sky. Most days, the jungle canopy gave us a false sense of night and day, as it held in the light. Today, however, we could see the coming dawn through the holes beginning to pierce the canopy.

To note some distinction between the farmers would be impossible. They were all pretty much the same height—short; they all wore the same colors and style of clothing—white or black cotton or silk, long-sleeved tops and long-legged pants, similar to a pair of pajamas, to reflect the sun and heat. Their oxen were even pretty much the same color. But there was something about Mya's family that allowed me to pick them out from amongst all the others. Each day as we approached the village, I would scan the fields hoping to see them, all three of them. I suppose they knew we were there, just as we knew the VC [Viet Cong] were there amongst them. As the nightly bombings increased, their pockmarked fields became less of a straight plow. Oxen and people alike skirted the craters, plowing around them, just another obstacle in life to be avoided. In many ways, the war was just a detour for them. If it disrupted their day, they just plowed around it. Life did not stop because the war interfered with their living. As the pockmarks increased, I began to leave an extra box or two of my C rations on the rock by which they sat every day for their own lunch break, if you could call it that. There was never much food passed around. Mostly Mya's mother would rub the shoulders of her husband—a small gesture of kindness. Mya would oftentimes crawl onto the rock and play her own version of Queen of the Mountain, stretching her arms into the air as far as she could reach. What was she reaching for? I used to wonder. A way out?" The hands of God to reach down and touch her and make all the pain of war go away? Who was she imploring to come to her aid?

One day, Mya's father and mother appeared to fall asleep, and Mya wandered off about the same time those in the field began their disappearing act. Mya ran with carefree abandon around the edge of the rice paddy, headed in our direction. Without a word, I jumped up and went after her. Scooping her up in my arms, we darted behind brush and bamboo stands, working our way around to where her family had been. Only minutes had lapsed, but in those few minutes, her family had disappeared, leaving their blanket behind. Grabbing the blanket, I wrapped Mya in it and made my way back to the trench.

Mya was frightened, as any child would be, but I couldn't have just left her out there. Opening a C ration, I gave her the crackers and cake from the tins. As soon as the fire fight stopped, I would find a way to return her to the village. At least that was my plan. I would probably be written up this time; I had been warned how many times in the past? That really was the least of my worries. How was I going to keep her safe? Of the many possibilities for what could happen, a miracle was high on my list.

I guess you could say I got that miracle—one of many, in fact. As the black pajamas began appearing out of the rice paddies, I glanced over to see Mya's mother and father standing at the edge of the village, calling for their daughter. Please, I whispered, please tell them she is safe, and I will return her to them as soon as I can.

That night's battle was no different than the others. We lost two soldiers, but our enemy lost at least forty. Still they came, multiplying like rats along the way. For every one of us, there were twenty of them. One could believe they were being spit out of the ground like ants. One falls, twenty take its place.

It would be morning before I could return Mya. I waited behind a bamboo stand for her family to come out into the fields. I knew they would be there;

they always were, just like clockwork. Life for these people was just that—clockwork. Steady paced and moving forward. Don't stop, or you'll fall behind. And so it was. They soon appeared, walking a little slower [than usual] this time. I handed Mya my box of C rations for the day and sat her down on the edge of the bank, knowing they would see her, and I quickly did a disappearing act of my own.

There is military protocol and rules and regulations that a soldier is to follow. I had broken any number of them, and I was soon to find out just how many. All I could respond with under the questioning by my CO [commanding officer] was, "Could you have left that child out there, knowing what was coming? Could you have sat by and watched as she was most certainly killed?" Knowing that he had children of his own, I knew his answer before he spoke it. How do you punish someone for doing something that was morally right and at the same time lawfully wrong?

Out on patrol a week later, we came upon Mya's field. You realize I didn't know her name yet, but when her parents had been calling for her, it sounded as if they were saying "Mya." So I had called her Mya and named this rice paddy *Mya's Field*. Our mission objective was changing, and this time we maneuvered closer to the village. Reports had come down that the VC were hiding within the village, making their appearance-and-disappearance act much easier to orchestrate. This was not a disorganized war, as many are; this was very much like a symphony—different sections of instruments, villagers and farmers, all being directed by the bandleader. Everyone chimed in at the correct time, and a symphony was born. Where the bandleader was now was the real question. How was he directing this orchestra? No one appeared to stand out and lead the symphony, but each section answered on cue. And music filled the air—not the strains of a beautiful violin, but the screams of RPGs as they made their way into the rice paddies. That day, we took our fight into the village as necessary to rout out Charlie. The villagers are willing to hide us both.

As we passed the rock on which I had first seen Mya standing, I noticed a small woven basket. Darting out of line, I grabbed it off the rock and opened it as we marched on. Rice and a small, delicate-looking flower. I was moved by the offering of rice. Rice to the farmers was like gold was to us. Rice was their sustenance; rice was their life bread and blood. I knew it was meant for me, for I had rescued and saved their daughter. The flower was their daughter, the bright spot in their life.

I am a soldier; I am trained to kill, but killing does not come naturally to me. How many times had I been told to focus on what was at hand, staying alive, rather than worry about these people?

We moved further north, and I doubted I would ever see Mya again. I would always remember her, though.

Mya: Thank you, Writer. I must go now. Father passed last year, and Mother is so lost without him. She is very old now, can hardly walk, but she keeps going into the fields looking for Father. I have to follow her everywhere. Your White Soldier comes even for us Vietnamese. You are surprised?

JC: *I am.*

Mya: Why, Writer? Do you not think we go to your same heaven?

JC: *I had not thought of it that way. I thought perhaps one of your dragons or fairies would come for you, as dragons and fairies are the main characters in your creation story. I thought the White Soldier came only for the soldiers.*

Mya: Your White Soldier comes for all souls who fight bravely in battle. There are no boundaries in war, just war and killing. And then every once in a while, someone kind like Joe comes through with his kindness and reminds us that we are all one in the Father's eyes.

JC: *Thank you, Mya.*

Mya: Thank you, Writer, for telling all of our stories.

Watching the Sun Rise

Narrated by Jeremiah from the other side, after he passed. Jeremiah wanted to share his only good memory of the war and chose not to reveal any other information about his passing, whether it happened during the war or after he'd returned home. At the time he experienced this particular sunrise, he was in Vietnam on R&R (rest-and-relaxation leave).

Note: This Jeremiah is neither Jeremiah C. in "Nine Heroes" nor Jeremiah S. in "A Covert Mission."

The sun is coming up, Writer. Can you see it? Can you feel its rays of warmth touch your skin? My body feels alive as I stand in its golden rays. It is a rare treat to get to see the sun. Being out in the jungle, we can't always see above or through the canopy, but this morning I can see and feel its warmth. I'm not in the jungle today; today is my R&R. I could be showering, washing and drying clothes, sleeping in, but no, I've come outside to watch the sun rise.

Back home I would be up every morning with the sun. That's the way it is on the farm—up every morning at the crack of dawn. Do you know why they call it the crack of dawn, Writer? Because when those first rays start to brighten the darkness, it is as if the sky is splitting open. The sky just cracks open like an egg, spilling out its orange yolk. At least that is what my dad told me. We used to go out with our cups of coffee and sit on the fence and watch the sun rise. I enjoyed that time with my dad. I didn't have it for long, but I sure did enjoy it.

Would be back there today if I hadn't gotten shipped off to war. I don't have it in my bones to kill, Writer. I couldn't even kill my old dog Skipper when he got so lame. I just don't have it in me to kill another living soul. I don't.

Sitting here with my coffee, I feel as if my dad were right here with me. Oh, but to be back on the farm! I will be back there soon, though. Not too many more days to go. Dad says he's got lots of chores waiting for me. Don't think I will ever grumble about chores again.

The sun is almost up over that ridge now, Writer. Guess I'd better go pack. My flight back to camp leaves soon. I didn't get everything done that I wanted to while I was away, but I was dry for a few days, and looky here, I got to sit this morning and watch the sun rise.

It won't be long now before I'm back in the steamy jungle heat, wet to my skin. Leeches sucking the life force out of me. But this morning, I think I'll sit here and rest in the sun. I don't have much to pack anyway. I'll just sit and rest a few minutes more.

It isn't as simple, this dying process. Not that we "die"; rather, we pass into, transition into, another existence, one of vibration. We are a million, billion, trillion little specks of light energy that swirl around and take form once again. If you had eyes that were accustomed to seeing energy fields or auras, you could see the spirit leave the body in a bright flash of energy. Just like that, with a whoosh, and we are gone. Only our physical shell remains.

. . . I'm getting short, Writer. Only three more months, then I'm homeward bound. Back to Cincinnati, home of the Cincinnati Reds. Maybe I can try out for the team finally. I'm a great baseball player, Writer; I have a pitching arm like you've never seen. If I hadn't been drafted, that is where I would be, pitching for the Reds. I'm a baseball player, not a killer. They tell us to justify the killing with saving our own life. In some instances, that makes sense. But when we go out on patrol and fire first, the logic leaves me. I ask forgiveness for every life I take, Writer—every life. At night, I cry for those I have killed during the day. If it were a different time and a different place, I would ask them to be my friend instead.

Everything we do here is so against the morals we were brought up with at home in the States. For some here, it seems as if they kill for the sport of it. They keep count as if it is a competition they can win. I'm not judging them, Writer. I'm really not. We each do what we have to do to get through the horror we see around us each day.

It is not hard to make friends here—just awkward, because you never know if tomorrow he will be gone, or perhaps you will. It is hard to lose a friend, one you may have only known for a day or less. War is truly a case of us all being in the same boat, with nowhere to sail. Soon my boat will be sailing for home; I can't wait. Come to think of it, dead or alive, I will return home in the end. I pray I return home alive. The first thing I will do is, yes, go to a Reds game. I have my game shirt, Writer, see? [*He lifted up his olive-drab green t-shirt to show me a red shirt underneath.*] I'm not supposed to be wearing it, but you won't tell. It is my good-luck charm. Pretty groady and stinky, as it doesn't get washed much but for a rain storm now and then, but maybe it smells bad enough to drive the evil spirits away. [*He laughed.*]

We get through each day, Writer, never taking another minute for granted. All we have for sure is the minute we are living through right now. Right this minute.

2

The White Soldier

"No one passes alone. No one passes alone."
Doyle Delbert Tory, my father

There is nothing clean or pretty about war. As the spirit soldiers told me how they passed in battle, my own spirit was out of my physical body and, via the world of spirit, experiencing their last moments with them. As each soldier told his story, I was an observer floating above the scene, seeing and hearing all that went on. As these men relived their events, I heard and felt their vibrations of horror. My heart and soul ached for each who passed out of the physical as I watched via the world of spirit.

As you will read in chapter 3, all of the men describe seeing "the White Soldier," the guise God takes when He meets soldiers passing out of their bodies and into the world of spirit. Before hearing the soldiers' stories, I had not considered that God could be anything but a single entity. Yet when more than one soldier passed, He was there for each of them. I realized that He is unlimited in what He can do and where He can be.

As I began to write Private Jeffery C.'s story, a figure appeared among the soldiers.[6] The fighting stopped as He stood before me in the middle of the bloody battlefield. He was resplendent in the white military mess dress uniform of all military services; decorations of every war, every conflict, and every military action adorned His left breast. Slowly His right hand rose to the edge of His military cap as He saluted me.

"Thank you. Writer," was all He said.

It was at that moment that I recognized Him, for I too had met God once before in His form of the White Soldier.

I didn't know who He was the day my father passed in 1961, the soldier in His shining white uniform, ribbons and medals all over His chest. But I saw Him over and over again that first night, as I stared at the ceiling reliving the angry words I had spoken to my father. I felt he had betrayed me; I had begged him

---

6 This was the first story I received from the soldiers.

not to go back to fly and finish training exercises with the U.S. Navy, but he hadn't listened. He had been killed the next day in one of those training exercises. He was thirty-seven, and I was ten.

After the day my father died, sleep eluded me for many nights, but still the White Soldier stood, watching over me. I would see Him again at my father's funeral and at the cemetery, standing among the many U.S. Navy men and women who attended Dad's burial. Perhaps I wasn't meant to recognize Him back then; perhaps I was meant to learn the lesson of trusting in a higher power. It would take many more years of self-reflection and soul searching before I would learn the lesson and trust again.

As I was gathering stories for this book, I shared my White Soldier story with my friend Chris, himself a veteran of Operation Desert Storm (1991–1992). Chris has given his permission for me to share a story his father told him upon his own return from service in Vietnam.

"I am almost forty years old and this story still gives me chills when I think about it," said Chris.

My father, who has passed now from a heart attack, told me some stories of this "White Soldier." He said many of his buddies, as well as he, had seen this specter. My father was a combat engineer in 'Nam and was in a five-ton [truck] when several of his buddies got shot through the tarp of the bed while travelling out to a FOB [forward operating base]. He and another soldier were the only two of thirteen who made it out alive.

> He said they had laid down and were returning fire, when out of the corner of his eye, he noticed an almost blinding white light behind him. His buddy turned and was about to fire, as they thought some VC had somehow gotten in behind them.
>
> It was the White Soldier. He lifted his hand to them like He was saying "stop," and then put His finger to His mouth as if to tell them shush and be quiet. He was crouched down next to the dead and dying soldiers and was comforting and holding them.
>
> My father and his buddy turned back around to the VC and started firing again. But they noticed that there was no return fire or anything. They didn't even see anyone out there anymore. When they turned back around, the White Soldier was gone. My father said it seemed like when the White Soldier had told them stop and be quiet, it was as if He had made the VC leave and quit firing on them, although when it happened at first, he thought that the White Soldier was telling them, "Stop, don't shoot me. Don't say anything. I am here to help."

3

Last Patrol

I realize how fragile life is in combat situations and the hurt you feel when you lose a comrade in arms. I served with a Vietnamese Airborne Battalion, and they were comrades in arms, and the feeling for them was the same as if it had been Americans being lost in battle.

Ralph, Phang Rang, Vietnam, 1968

The hero soldiers whose stories are a part of this chapter are real. Their names, their deaths, and their stories are real. But there is absolutely no way to prove that these men existed.

Each man who stepped forward to tell a story gave me his rank, name, date of death, and the location where he passed. However, I have excluded some identifying information so that I might protect their privacy.

Nine Heroes

The following nine accounts are from soldiers who passed in Vietnam between 1965 and 1975.

Private First Class Jeremiah C., Hanoi

He came for me, your White Soldier. I told Him to go away, to find someone else who was worthy to be taken home by none other than God Himself. But He just stood there, waiting.

Men were dying all around me, carnage everywhere. Blood as thick as molasses covered the ground. I'm a country boy, Writer; I'm just a country boy. I wasn't made for all this killing. I used to ask myself every morning, "Why am I here?" Every morning I asked, and still I received no answer. I guess I don't have to ask any more now, do I? It's over—it's all over. I'm going home. Mom and Pop will bury my body on the farm, under the old oak. Most of the family is already there—Grandma and Grandpa, my brother Jimmy. I guess we will finally get to be together again.

He's still here, Writer, just waiting. Why won't He go on? Why won't He just leave me to my shame?

Let my body and soul just stay here on this bloody field of dreams. We all had dreams, you know. Most of us [were] just out of high school. I couldn't afford college, but I had me a job at Mr. Ray's feed store for the summer. Give me time to figure out just what I wanted to do. I knew Pop needed me on the farm, and I was planning to split my time working between the farm and the feed store. Come fall, I was hoping to take a class or two at the local college. No one knew it, but I wanted to be a lawyer one day. I had to figure out a way to do that, money being short and all. Guess I won't be using my GI Bill now, will I? That was the carrot they dangled in front of all us country boys: come fight for us, and we will send you to college when it's over. It was a good carrot, made our getting drafted feel better. They knew it was an empty promise, though, because most of us would die before getting to use it. In the end, if I had made it, it would have been the way I could have become a lawyer. Maybe next time around.

Everyone's falling around me, Writer. [There are] White Soldiers everywhere, picking up bodies, takin' them home. He's still standing there, though. He's waitin' on me. Why? He can feel my pain, my anguish. He knows what I did. He knows my sin. Yet there He is, waiting for me.

Writer, when will the pain stop? Will the memory ever go away? Will anyone know what I did? Bullets were flying everywhere. I didn't see Johnny comin' up behind me. I just heard the noise, felt the movement of air. I was already pulling the trigger when I realized it was him. Will they know it was me, or will they just think we were both casualties of the battle?

Private Harry H., Saigon

Triple H or Harry the Third they called me. Yes siree, what a day that was, June fourth. No sooner had I been awakened by the first shirt [the first sergeant] when disaster struck. Volley after volley of rounds fell on our camp. Not much to protect us. Foxholes, if we could get to them fast enough; bunkers, if we could even get in their shadow. No, pretty much we were just sittin' ducks. Lots of White Soldiers that day. Maybe one of us made it out. Don't rightly remember seeing Patrick after the melee started. Haven't seen him up here, so guess he might have been the only lucky ones that day. His girlfriend, Jenny, had just sent him a four-leaf clover that week. He was so happy the day he got that letter. Held up the clover wrapped in cellophane and said, "This is from my Jenny. She's my four-leaf clover." Maybe she was more luck than she knew.

So many things I wish I had the opportunity to do over again. One shouldn't die with regrets. You have to live your life to the fullest. Live each day as if it were the last, perhaps then one would be more grateful, more appreciative when they wake up the next day. Each day was a gift here, the waking-up part. Some days you just didn't know if you were going to survive it or not. Then you catch a couple hours (if that) of sleep, and you are awake again. We were constantly putting our asses on the line. Only stopped for two reasons: (1) you were dead or

(2) you were lucky enough to be rotating out. Three more weeks, and I would have been one of the lucky ones leaving, rotating out. Three weeks, twenty-one more days, and a wake up. Guess my wake up came earlier than expected.

Stay cool, Writer, we appreciate that you are hearing us. Be grateful for every day you wake up.

PRIVATE LEONARD C., BIEN HOA

There isn't much to say. Sometimes you are here, and then you are gone. Pretty much that is how it happened for me.

I was on patrol, and my buddy, Jim, was off to my right. I never even saw what hit me, but I heard him [the enemy soldier]. Rather, I heard the branch crack as he stepped on it. I swung around just as I saw a flash of light. The last thing I heard was the click of the trigger as that gook pulled it.[7] My last prayer was for Jim, that he didn't come over and try to help me. "Stay where you are Jim," I silently prayed. "No need for both of us to die today."

I don't think I died instantly; my body sort of went into suspended motion. Not much I could see or hear, but I didn't feel dead. I tried to move my arm, but if it moved, I didn't feel it. I just lay there, staring up at the dark sky. Then I saw the strangest thing—a light lit up the night sky, and there He was, the White Soldier. He was coming for me after all. Some of the guys talked about having seen Him when deep in battle. I guess they were the lucky ones, just put on notice, perhaps, that their time was near, or maybe that they had escaped death at that time. He saluted me and bent down to pick me up.

I hope Jim finds my letter. I wanted to ask him if he could see the light. It was so bright. I hope it

7 *Gook* is a derogatory term for Asians in general.

is only the dying who sees it. So many people have died. There is a camaraderie here that only a soldier knows. We are brought together out of fear, yet when one of us dies, there is a love that surges forth for that brother whether or not we were kin.

JC: *Leonard, is it a fear of death or fear of the unknown?*

Ma'am, it is both and a lot more. Most of us were just young boys, perhaps young adults, though we were just out of high school, barely had a chance to experience life outside of the classroom. Dropped in a country that we had never heard of, told to kill anything that moved before it killed us. How does one live with themselves after killing another human being? What were we even fighting for over here? I saw young boys over here carrying rifles. How do you kill someone who is younger than your youngest brother? It was kill or be killed. I so wanted to have compassion for each of the enemy I met, yet it was him or me. Did they want to kill us as much as we didn't want to kill them? I had no hatred for this person I was told was my enemy. Was it the same for them? We were so ill prepared. There were so many innocent lives lost on both sides. Everyone lost a son to war. In Vietnam, they lost women and children as well. In America, it was the women and children who suffered when soldiers returned home and were unable to stop reliving the horrors of war.

Jim, I hope you find this letter, man. I know you made it home. Have a beer for me, will you man?

PRIVATE FIRST CLASS THOMAS R., DA NANG

I guess it is my turn. I've been hanging back, letting everyone else go. They fought in the war; I never made it to the war. Our transport was shot down before we even made the LZ [landing zone].

I hadn't been in-country yet, flying in a MATS [Military Air Transport Service] cargo aircraft across the Pacific. It was in Seoul [South Korea] where I boarded the transport for my last leg over to Vietnam. We were shot down over the South China Sea as we were on approach to Da Nang. No one even saw it coming. We just felt the blast and the shudder of the transport before falling out of the sky. White Soldiers everywhere, Writer, everywhere. There must have been hundreds, one for each of us it seemed. There were none of us left to feel the impact of the plane on the water. We were all gone by then.

I guess my last letter won't make it home, will it, Writer?[8] It is still here in my pocket. How many families will never know how much their sons loved them? For in the end, that is what we write

8 U.S. soldiers were instructed to write a "last letter home" to their family in case of their death. I don't know the history behind this practice, but I assume it was part of the army's standard operating procedure, because even I was instructed to write a last letter home while I served in the army (see the afterword). Several of my friends who went to Vietnam and returned have talked about being required to write their last letter home and being thankful that it never had to be sent.

about, isn't it? We forget all the bad times and only remember the good times, so they will know that we were thinking good thoughts about them when our time was up. At least that is what my letter was about—all the good times, all the things I was grateful for during those childhood to teen years. Who would have thought I would never see my family again or have children to bounce on my pa's knees? My ma was countin' on that—for me to have the grandkids, that is.

You just don't think like that when you are leaving to come here. You hope against hope that you will be coming home; you don't plan to die here. If you did plan to die, then you would be a quitter. Sometimes, remembering all the things you planned to do—college, marriage, have kids—those are the thoughts that get you through the war, through those nights and days when all you do is pray that it isn't your day to go.

Is anyone ever truly ready when that day comes? I wasn't ready, Writer. I wasn't ready. So many things I would have done differently, so many more things I would have said when I had the chance. That last night in Seoul, I called home. Ma was away at her church meeting, but Pa was there. We talked man to man. Haven't done that since we last went deer hunting.

I couldn't ever kill a deer, you know. I just went because it was time I could spend with my pa. His last words to me were, "I'm proud of you son." I told him how much I loved him and Ma. You never know when your words may be the last, so it gives you cause to always tell them you love them, no matter how hard it is or the kind of life you've experienced.

Staff Sergeant Thomas C., Saigon[9]

"Morgan, get over here!" was the last thing I heard before I felt the sting of the bullet, and my leg went numb.

"I'm coming Lieutenant, I'm coming." If I kept repeating it over and over, perhaps my body would listen and do what I was telling it to do. There was a swarm of people crowding around the chopper, all trying to get on at once. Bodies dangled off the struts as she tried to rise in the air. Like a phoenix she was, trying to rise out of the ashes of death and destruction.

Feet—it felt like millions of tiny feet running over my body. Why didn't anyone stop and help me? Couldn't they see I was hurt? Why didn't anyone stop and help me? Lieutenant? Where is the lieutenant? Why hasn't he come for me? Mass confusion everywhere. The swarm is buzzing, crying out in words I don't understand. But the energy of the swarm, the fear—the fear is making it buzz louder and louder.

I can no longer see the chopper; I can only hear her straining to break free of this massive swarm. The blades turn faster and faster and then settle into her customary rhythm as she pulls free from the swarm. The phoenix has risen once again, flying

9 It is my belief that Staff Sergeant Thomas C. was in Saigon at the city's fall, as part of the landing party near the site of the former U.S. embassy, the last place of American presence in Vietnam.

free into the sky—this time without me, for I have been swallowed up by the swarm. Will they turn on me like they did her? Will I be next? Is their fear such that they will not remember all the good things I did for them—the candy sent from home that I shared with their children, the beds I have shared with their daughters, the smiles I shared with the old men, neither of us understanding what the other was saying, but both understanding the smile between us.

The swarm was turning now; the same tiny feet that ran over my body before have retreated over me again. The street is quiet now. Where have they gone? Where does a swarm of people caught up in fear go?

All is silent for just a moment. Off in the distance I hear her. Is she returning for me? Did the lieutenant realize I wasn't aboard?

No longer is she olive-drab green; rather, she is now a soft white, fuzzy white, like a ghost ship returning through the fog.

"Oh no," I think. The swarm—if they see you, they will all be coming back again.

But they don't see you, do they? Only I can see you. You are coming for me; it must be my time to go.

The ghost bird settles on the pockmarked road, and the pilot emerges, dressed in His white mess dress. There is no sound, no running feet, no swarm of people. Just me and the pilot.

"Staff Sergeant, it's time to go, son. We don't want to be late for sunrise now do we?" Bending down, the pilot picks me up and carries me to the ghost bird. He straps me into the copilot's seat, and I have a bird's eye view of the crack of dawn as we fly right into it. I have seen both the phoenix and the sun rise twice today. The first I watched, the second I am part of.

SERGEANT LEONARD M., DA NANG

I guess you are wondering if I am related to the Jeffery C. who came to you when the children had gathered together.[10] Yes, I am his brother—stepbrother actually. I am the older of the two. My father married his mother and adopted her two children as his own and raised them. I was already over here when Jeffery showed up. We weren't in the same platoon, though we were stationed close to one another. Our roles here were different. I worked with the big guns, the artillery unit, while Jeffery worked with a special ops (operations) group.

We had a reunion of sorts when Jeffery arrived—a short one anyway. I'm not sure how we ended up in the same hellhole together, but we did. I can only imagine the agony Mom and Dad went through when they had to send both of us off to war. It isn't just the soldier that participates in the war; it is the family also. We may be the one that experiences the dangers of war, but our families experience the heartache and emotions of war. A war changes everyone, not only those that are directly involved, but also those that wait back home for them to

---

10 Jeffery C. is the name of the soldier who appeared to me while I was speaking with the spirit children in 2011 (see the introduction). He was also a member of the patrol at the heart of "A Covert Mission," whose stories are told later in this chapter. He and Leonard had the same last name.

return. How hard it must have been for Mom and Dad to know both their sons were in danger.

War changes a young man, it surely does. The only things I ever shot and killed before coming here were deer and elk, maybe a rabbit now and then. I didn't have to look them in the eyes like I do these people. These are people, human beings just like me. They are the brothers and sons of moms and dads here, in this land. They are here to defend what is theirs. What are we here defending?

I had been thinking about Jeffery that morning, wondering how he was doing, when we were called out. Another unit's patrol had come across an NVA [North Vietnamese Army] base and had them pinned down. We located the patrol's location and started raining in the mortars and artillery on the NVA base. Time stood still that day. While we fired on the NVA camp, some of the NVAs had scooted around and gotten above the patrol, and they were taking it from both sides by NVAs. They were trapped in the valley, and we were doing our best to fire in both directions.

Ammo was running low, and the day was wearing on. The afternoon rains came at their appointed time. Funny how the only thing that was on time in this war was the rain. Nothing we wore had a chance to dry out between storms; we were forever wet. The rain dampened our spirits, just as it dampened everything underneath it. There was a lull in the firing, and I stole a moment to look off to the West.

The sun would be setting soon. Her orange glow had followed the rains. I don't know what hit me. I saw the sun, orange, bright, and glowing. As I smiled, it exploded in front of my face.

It was then that I saw them coming towards me the White Soldier and Jeffery. The White Soldier carried Jeffery. Both of their uniforms were covered in blood—more blood than I thought a body could hold. The White Soldier laid Jeffery on the ground and saluted me. Together, we walked off to the west. I carried Jeffery this time, and the White Soldier walked beside me in case I fell.

JC: *Leonard, Jeffery doesn't speak of the White Soldier in his letter. Do you know why?*

Jeffery didn't know God, Ma'am, not like I did anyways. But I knew God is faithful and that even if we don't know Him, He does watch out for us, and He will send His angels to bring us home. All of us. This time He came for Jeffery and me.

JC: *Thank you, Leonard.*

"The next three soldiers served together on a single mission and all died on the same mission.

Sergeant Christopher M., Da Nang

"Roger two-niner, incoming at three o'clock." Static sputtered, and the radio call was barely audible.

"Repeat Roger three-four, repeat." Only silence answered.

We heard them long before we could see them, the chopper blades making their characteristic *thuwack-thuwack-thuwack.* The landing zone in front of us had been cleared of shrubs and vines; with luck, they would be able to touch down long enough to unload their human cargo. Already, men were crawling out to the struts, getting ready to jump. You had to be fast to get off, out, and away, before Charlie had time to get you in his sight and pull the trigger.

Most of these greenhorns would have practiced the unloading maneuver at least a couple times back at base camp. Still, all the practice in the world didn't make it any easier when your heart was racing 180 miles per hour, the ground was coming up at 125 mph, and there was still six feet to drop.

"Three, two, one jump!" could just barely be heard over the *thuwack-thuwack-thuwack.* Bodies jumped and rolled for the perimeter cover. Usually the maneuver went off without a hitch; everyone was out and belly-crawling towards our position, another successful drop of reinforcements.

I glanced down for just a moment as a green snake slithered through my legs. Damn snakes. At least they aren't poisonous, just jaw-dropping until you recognize its characteristic tail end, which looks as if it has been dipped in paint. The one without the painted tail is the poisonous one.[11]

The increasing speed of the blades brought my eyes back up to the chopper.

"Oh shit, man, cover me," I said to Tom, and I ran as low as I could to the chopper.

A damn soldier had dropped all right, but his ruck strap was caught on the strut. He would soon be lifted up with the bird, a dangling target for Charlie, dead within seconds. The crewman saw me coming and looked down, realizing the emergency. We both dove at the same moment as gunfire erupted from the other side of the LZ. Grabbing the strap, I yanked as the chopper rotated up just enough to loosen the strap. Thankfully, our patrol had returned fire, giving us just enough time to almost crawl back to cover.

I felt the first sting in my left lower leg, then my side. My leg felt as if it were exploding. Crawling was more like trying to drag my body along. Ten more feet, just ten more feet. The new guy had

---

11 I have not been able to identify this snake with the "painted tail."

made it; the guys had pulled him over the edge and into cover. I wasn't so lucky. Another volley of shots rang out. After the first two, I didn't feel anything anymore. I could see my leg, a bloody, mangled looking mess. As I sat up, my body stayed behind. I had arms and hands that seemed to work, but nothing else did. It was all so strange. I looked around as Charlie overran the landing zone. They ran right past me.

"Hey guys, can't you see me?" I called out. But no one heard, they just kept running. Good I thought, we can box them in. I can fire from behind them while the patrol takes them out from the front. Boy, they were stupid to make that mistake.

"Stupid, stupid Charlie," I chanted. Reaching for my M-16, my hand passed right through the butt. Huh? I tried again—nothing. I couldn't be dead. I had a body, or so it seemed. I could talk and sing. No one else could hear me, but I could hear myself. What was going on?

Then a presence filled the space around me, and He appeared, the White Soldier. Others had spoken of seeing Him as He came to get their fallen buddies. Now He appeared to be coming for me. I guess I was dead, but I sure felt like I was alive. Couldn't run anywhere or pick up my weapon, but I felt alive.

"Come on, son, it's time to go," He said, reaching down to pick up my body.

That's the last thing I remember, Writer, the last thing. I guess, in the end, I was a hero after all, wasn't I, Writer?"

JC: *Yes, Christopher, you are a hero.*

Staff Sergeant Matthew R., Da Nang

They call me Hollywood because I look just like James Broderick, the movie star. Slicked back hair, sideburns until they shaved them off, the jaunty walk—I had it all. Made me feel good, them thinkin' I was someone special.

Didn't last for long though. Nothing does when you are in the jungle. More important things to worry about, like surviving. Back home I was a dandy with the ladies. Here too, actually. We get R&R, and I headed straight for town. Girls as thick as barflies on a summer's day. They were fallin' over themselves to sit at my table. Cost me a few dollars to take them home for the night. To them that few dollars is a year's worth of rice. Those girls were the richest people when we left 'Nam, the new class of millionaires. They should have been anyway. They had the only commodity worth selling, and they didn't even have to really sell it. Keep the GI happy, that is all they had to do.

One young, sweet thing I visited often. Rose she said to call her. Rose said they saw themselves not as prostitutes, rather as patriots (my word, not hers, you wouldn't understand her word), heroes. They believed they were doing service for their country, just as their soldiers out fighting were. They saw it as a duty to serve, and made us forget about the girls we left back home. They helped us forget about a lot of things. In return we cherished those few hours we had away from the jungle and the war that raged on there. Just to be able to be clean and dry, if even just for twenty-four hours. It was all worth it.

"Hollywood, get your head down man," the lieutenant grunted. We were pretty strung out across a low-lying ridge, having just finished protecting a chopper drop of new recruits to add to the team. Our job was to get them back to camp so they could be reassigned. Got them all in, even the goofy kid at the end. Lost my buddy Chris[12] doing it, though. Had to leave him there; too hard to carry and shoot at the same time. Whether or not you ever believed in God, or somebody up there pulling strings, whatever name He goes by, when you had to leave your buddy behind, you prayed that there was someone and they would take the body fast, before the gooks got to it.

No one should have their body desecrated in the horrific way they treated the body of an American soldier. In retaliation, we did the same. I didn't, but I knew of men that did. Gooks got us from the middle and the end. Pushed us right into their fire trap, and none of us were going to make it out alive. Kenny might have made it out; no one has seen him here yet. Don't know how he might have survived the hell, but maybe he did. Maybe he was far enough ahead of the rest of us that when the big guns opened up,

12 Christopher M., see page 48.

he was already through the trap and headed back to camp.

Pretty bad for the new recruits too. First day in-country, survive the chopper drop, and then lose their lives on the way back to camp. Full rucks and all. They didn't have a chance. They fought well, scared to death, weren't seasoned like us. Dumb mistakes—mistakes a greenhorn makes. Hope they had their letters in their pockets. Not much left of a body to reclaim, but maybe we would be lucky and someone would find us.

Perhaps our last letters never got back to our families. At least we felt good writin' them. Even if things back home with the parents was bad, the thought of dying without saying goodbye was worse. Sometimes fences got mended that seemed broken when we left, just by writin' the letter. Me, I was good with my parents. We didn't always see eye-to-eye, but I do miss them. My letter was pretty short; just told each one how much I loved them and I hoped to see them again. If they were receiving that letter, there was no seeing them again until they showed up here. I knew that. Just wanted to give them something to hope for. We weren't a religious family, never set foot in a church 'ceptin' for Grandpa's funeral. But as I said before, over here, you pray there is a god somewhere who loves you enough to get you out of this hell.

Well, Writer, it's time to go. I did see the White Soldier—lots of White Soldiers, in fact. There were a lot of us going home that day. Blink of an eye, and we were gone. Kind of strange to leave our bodies behind. They were just shells after all.

My buddy Donny told me, "Your body is just a shell to protect your soul and your spirit. Just a shell. You gotta treat that shell good, man. Treat that shell good." Guess he was right.

But I'm here, and there is a bridge, Writer—a big beautiful bridge lit by all the colors of the rainbow. We all gather when a family member comes across, and we are there to greet them, just like you tell everyone. Of course, here now, we are one big family. When you are part of a war, everyone is your family as you bond together. You look out for one another, even in the end.

We'll all come to greet you, Writer, but your time isn't for quite a while yet. Just keep taking our stories. We will see you soon enough.

Private First Class John M., Da Nang

Hey, Writer, I've been waiting to meet you. Finally, it is my turn.

I had my last letter—you know all about those. Wrote it on the chopper with Leonard.[13] We flew in together at the beginning of our tour nine months ago. We got separated upon arrival. That sounds pretty fancy, doesn't it? "We flew in together," like we were some rich dudes flying in to some private vacation spot in our private jet.

It wasn't like that though, was it, Writer? We were scared to death. There was no excitement there in the chopper that night. Fear rode with us all the way in. Crew master briefed us as we were approaching the LZ. I'm not a prayin' man, Writer, but I prayed that night. I prayed so hard and fast. Then it was time. Crew master called "jump," and we did—as fast as we could tumble out of that bird, we did. Felt like we were jumping into a pool of boiling water. That humidity hit us like a ton a bricks. When you are in the jungle, the canopy overhead captures all that moisture and traps it underneath. We made it in, though—all of us. The guys were waiting for us and got us in safely. It would be a long night, and morning would come even quicker. So much to learn that can't be taught in a classroom. OJT [on-the-

13 Leonard M., see page 45.

job training] they call it, OJT. You learn it all right there, every second of every day.

Camp wasn't too bad; we just bunked in with whoever wasn't there that first night. There'd be plenty of time to build a hooch [a shelter of sorts, not grand in design, just enough to get out of the elements (rain, sun) and afford some protection] in the morning. Right now, we just needed to sleep. Perhaps we would find it was all just a bad dream when we woke up in the morning. Streaks of red were beginning to pierce that black sky when I finally shut my eyes.

"Hey man, get up." Opening my eyes, I saw the butt of an M-16 suspended midair.

"I guess we're not in Kansas anymore are we?" I said to myself.

No sooner had I grabbed my ruck and scrambled out then the soldier who had wakened me crawled in and was already asleep. I would learn quickly to grab every minute of sleep I could, even standin' on my feet, if need be. Sleep was that precious out here in the jungle.

Didn't take us long to get our orders. Quick introductions around, a spot for our hooch, and then we were assigned to our patrols. Just like the factory I used to work in, everything had an order to it. It was needed in the factory so people didn't get hurt. That same order was needed in the jungle so we didn't die. One wrong step, one wrong move here, and they were shipping your body, if anything was left of it, home in a box.

Bobby had come back home that way, in a box. There wasn't much left of him to begin with. Not sure why they didn't just leave him over here. Would have been kinder for his family. I hope they left me here, Writer, if there was nothing left of me.

I think some of the guys were grateful to see us new guys arrive. Gave them a chance to get some R&R, if even for a day or two. After you have been here, been on the line day in and day out, even a break for a day seems like a week away, though you never escape from all the shelling. It rings in your ears day and night.

My mom tried to get me to become a Boy Scout, said it would make a man out of me. I told her no way was I going to be one of those sissy Boy Scouts. I had no pa, so I didn't want to go showin' up with her all the time. They did lots of fun stuff, though. Bobby and his dad joined, took me on a few outings with them. Too bad we didn't go camping more often. That's what we did here, sort of camped out. Food was in cans; meat, crackers, dessert of some sort—all in cans [C rations]. By the time you got to eat, you pretty much didn't care what you were eating; anything tasted good.

Coffee on the other hand was like gold. For me, the smell of coffee was what took me home. Mom always had a pot of coffee on the stove. As soon as I would smell it in the morning, I would tumble out of bed to go downstairs and sit with her. It was our time together before our day began. I hope to be home soon, Writer, so I can sit with Mom and tell her all about my day away.

I had been in-country for nine months, had only three more to go. First Shirt counseled us all about getting short-timer attitude. There wasn't a place for it on the line.

"The only time you get short-timer attitude is when you are in the bird flying out of here," he'd say.

I tried not to get it, Writer, I really did. But I was gettin' short, and all I could think about was gettin' back home. Home, where I could be dry—just to be dry. There was nothing about me that was dry out here. I lived in perpetual wetness. "The ultimate wet dream experience," as some guys called it. With all the rain and steam from the jungle, there just wasn't a time when anything was dry. You couldn't afford to sleep without your boots on in case of a mortar attack, yet if you didn't, your feet never got dry. Some guys' skin was so wet it was sloughing off. Don't even try to imagine it, Writer. It was like a horrible dream. Living in the jungle was my version of living in hell. If the gooks didn't get you, the jungle conditions would.

Two weeks and a wake up to go, and I would be out of here. Rumor had it that the war was windin' down and we would all be going home soon, some sooner than expected. Rotations out were coming every day now, and oftentimes we would go out on patrol and come back to find empty hooches. Notes tacked on them from our friends read, "No time to say goodbye, man. I'm going home."

Last day—it had finally come. I was going home the next day, all in one piece, without the box. Anything I could leave behind for whoever was left, I did. Kind of a passing of the torch, so to speak. Not much we were going to need any more once we got stateside. Might as well leave it here for someone else to use.

"Grab your rifle, man. Jones can't go, and we need another body," the lieutenant said running past me.

"No, Lieutenant, I'm going home tomorrow," I said, all the while grabbing my pot [steel helmet], M-16, and ammo and heading out. Tapping my pocket, I made sure I could hear the crinkle of my letter. Wet as it was, that crinkle sound was still there.

You know most of the story from Christopher and Matthew's letters, so there is nothing new I can add to what happened that day. We'd gone up to the LZ to escort some new replacements in. They had gotten off the hill and under cover. The chopper left, stirring up a dust storm. When it settled, we took fire from all sides. We fell like matchsticks, Writer. Or maybe it is dominoes. You stand them all on their end and then push one, and it takes out everyone behind it. I fought hard because I was going home the next day, just a wake-up left. I had come too far and lived through hell not to go home.

Most of us, we didn't know what hit us. Fire rained down, and then it was light—a bright light. I saw Him, Writer, the White Soldier. He saluted me and then held out His hand to me, just an old country boy. I tried to stand and salute Him back, but nothing moved. There were so many of us that day. Some He carried. Others carried their buddies. Some of us just got in behind and followed Him. It didn't matter to where, just so long as it was away from here.

I saw my body, and I left it behind. It looked pretty good laying there, not too much blood. I guess if they found it, they shipped it home in a box after all. So either way, Writer, I went home that day.

Look, the sun is coming up over the ridge. Do you see it, Writer? Do you see it?

JC: *Yes John, I see it. It's time to wake up now. You are home John. You are home.*

A Covert Mission

The following stories are from four of ten heroes who passed in Vietnam while on a covert mission, an extremely sensitive military operation. Had the event for which this group of soldiers trained been carried out, the result would have been catastrophic.

Exposing this mission was not my goal, and this book is not about the politics of the war. I simply agreed to write these men's stories so their families will know they are safe in heaven, as well as in the hearts and minds of those they left behind. What they thought about in those last moments reflects their wishes and regrets.

All of these men passed in Da Nang on the same day, June 15, 1971. Jim D., who tells his story in "Four Dog Tags," later in this chapter, was also a member of the team sent on this mission.

Jeffery C.

Not everyone was out of Da Nang, and the war was not over by any means. Some of us were still deep within the jungles of 'Nam.

Have you ever been to war, Writer? Have you ever been so afraid that you couldn't move? Have you ever experienced the moment when you felt—known, actually—that the next bullet was meant for you? When, in a split second, you only thought of the ones you loved, your family back home—the family you wouldn't get to say "I love you" to before leaving them?

How many months had I been in the jungle before this last mission? Only the stick knew.[14] We carried them with us. They became our solace at night if we even got to stop hiding long enough to find sleep. Sleep was never as sound as it had been at home when we were just teenage boys out having fun at the pond or working on cars. Our life was stolen from us long before we even reached the jungle of 'Nam.

I didn't grow up learning to hate or experiencing the hatred of a people I did not know. I never even

14 Jeffery is referring to what is called a short-timer stick, used by soldiers to carve or mark the number of days in-country until the day they left. The stick was often passed onto the soldier taking the departing soldier's place, or carried home with him as a reminder of the time spent in Vietnam. Short-timer sticks came in all shapes and sizes and were oftentimes indicative of the unit the soldier was assigned to.

knew where Vietnam was or why we were fighting the Viet Cong until we landed there in the dark of night, on a hill surrounded by jungle.

"Welcome to hell," the first sergeant said. "Welcome to hell."

He was right—it was hell. Not the one you were taught to fear as a child; rather, hell of a people's own making. It was not necessarily of the Vietnamese people's own making; rather, it was my own government's fear of communism that brought me here. Fight the Viet Cong, free the Vietnamese. Yet I learned that on many levels the Viet Cong and the Vietnamese were all one and the same. So long as one had food to eat, it didn't matter what side they fought on. It was just a matter of which hand was going to feed you that day.

We wrote our last letter home flying in on the chopper. It was sealed and stashed away in our breast pocket before we even landed. I only hope my letter made it home. If not, this is the next best thing.

> Dad, Mom, Judy, I love you. I'm safe now. I can sleep with both eyes closed, and I am surrounded by peace. The outer war is over. I am Home. I'll be waiting for you; you still have a few years.

Thank you Writer. It is time to go. Got to make rounds. Some habits just don't seem to go away. Got to check on my men.

JEREMIAH S.

The sergeant told me to make sure I had a letter written to my folks back home in my pocket. I didn't have no folks to write to. So I wrote a letter to God.

> Dear God,
>
> I don't know if you know me or not, but my name is Jeremiah. I don't want to die, not like this, not way off here in this foreign land. If it is my time, make it quick, please, God. I've tried to be a good man, to do the right thing each time given my circumstances. I hope it is enough.
>
> Signed,
>
> Jeremiah

Didn't know where they would send it when it came time, but at least I had written my letter home. Life was so uncertain here. You didn't count the days you were alive; you were grateful for the seconds. Each one was so precious. Life continuously flashed in front of us. We tried not to dwell on it. We tried to just keep our head down and move forward. There was no time to daydream about home.

First Sergeant told us, "Those letters are your good luck charms. You don't want us to have to send that letter home, so stay safe." Everyone carried a good luck charm or two. Never could have too many. Many of us carried crosses or a rabbit's foot. Just think how many rabbits have to die each time a war breaks out, just so we can carry their feet and believe they will bring us good luck and keep us safe from Charlie. I carried both a cross and a rabbit's foot and, of course, my letter home. Didn't do any good though, did it? I'm still here [in heaven]. I'm glad Tommy K. was short and couldn't come with us.[15]

We were out on patrol when Charlie hit us, just came out of nowhere. They were like that you know. They just seemed to materialize out of the mists that settled in the jungle valleys. None of us had a chance.

Not sure who found our bodies; we were long gone by that time. We were on a special mission, only the captain knew what for. The rest of us just followed orders. I wonder what they did with my letter to God. I knows I don't have folks to send my letter to, but maybe somebody will remember me.

Yes, there were angels—at least I thought they were angels. Who was I to think that God would come for me? *White Soldiers* we called them. They came in white dress uniforms, medals all over their chest. Amidst all that blood and gore, they came in white uniforms to take us home. They were there and had been through every war, every battle. That's how we knew death was coming; we saw the White Soldiers and just knew it would be our time to go.

---

15 Tommy K. shares his story in "Four Dog Tags," later in this chapter.

Others had spoken of seeing them and lived through it, but not me, not this time. We didn't stop fighting when we saw them; we fought harder, anything to make them go away. In the end, we just laid down our rifles, stood, and saluted them—our last act. The battle was over.

All my buddies were there. Johnny, Mike, Floyd, Harold, and Skeeter—we called him that because he shot at everything that moved, had us jumpin' all the time. They all came to meet me. They couldn't have gotten there much earlier than me; we was all together that night. There must be a lot of White Soldiers working for God 'cause we sure kept them busy in 'Nam.

War is hell, and hell is war. Hey, who is that I see? Tommy, what are you doing here, man? I thought you were goin' home.

"I am home, so are you," said Tommy.

Rodney M.

You hesitate, Writer. You are getting the whole patrol, that is true. We are all here together and have chosen to come through for you. Just take our stories, Writer. The rest will follow.

You wanted to know about the spirits of the place, whether or not we saw them. I did. I saw and heard them. Each night when I lay down to sleep, they started. The anguish, the wailing of women and children. The utterings of old men and young men not old enough to die. The horrors of the war. The blood of Vietnam's people leached into the soil and remained active, even after they had passed. All asked the same question, "Why? Why have you invaded our land, destroyed our homes, our way of life? Who were you to judge what was best for our country? Why are you here?"

I had no answers for them, Writer. No answers. I didn't even know why I was here. Drafted into a war, half a continent away, to a land I had never even heard of before I got my draft notice. "To halt the spread of communism"—that is what I was told I was here for. In reality, we were just here to kill anything in black that moved—man, woman, or child. I couldn't kill the children; they were children, for God sakes. I knew some of them packed bombs, not afraid to lose their own life. They were taught that it was honorable to die young; great rewards awaited them in the afterlife. The young women were different; they used us just as we used them, though our intentions were much different. They used us for our money; we used them for their bodies. Not having any [women] of our own kind in-country, we made use of what was provided so graciously by our host. I didn't feel good about it. Not much about the war I felt good about.

In many ways, death so far away from home was justified because of my sins. And of sins, I had many. I often wonder how my life would have been had this war not interrupted it. Would I have found love and married and had a family of my own? I love kids. How many would I have had? They told us not to think about home and our families when we came through basic training. Said it would take our mind off our business, make us homesick, and get us killed. I guess in the end, they were right. My inability to shoot a child got us all killed.

Our patrol was ambushed from behind, but it all started with the child that appeared, dirty face and snotty nose, barefoot, walking right out of the bamboo stand and into our patrol. I was the first to see him. Had I shot him, he wouldn't have had time yell out our location. Paul shot him, did what I couldn't do. But it was too late. My failure to act is what got us killed.

Each of us has a piece to add of how it happened that day. It wasn't textbook—nothing about this war is textbook. That is why we are all coming through, so we can each give you our piece of the puzzle and you can see the whole picture, share the whole story of the mission from which no one would return. The picture is much more complex than just a simple killing of a patrol in the jungle far from home. This was a top-secret mission. I knew better than anyone what one mistake could mean. We died (figuratively) so many times in those steamy hot jungles; I'm surprised that it took the Viet Cong that long to finally get us. We lost all hint of innocence. The things we had to do just to survive. Nothing justified the horror we experienced.

At home, we were never taught to be grateful for each day; we learned that here in the jungle. Sometimes when the fighting got so bad, we prayed for another minute of life and were grateful for that minute, even if it brought death with the next one. It was in the quiet time, when we weren't out on patrol. But when we were back in camp, supposed to be sleeping—that is when we tried to justify the killing. Kill or be killed—it was that simple. Live or die. None of us wanted to die, at least not like this, far away from our home and family.

See, Writer, I just wanted you to know about our life here. I wasn't afraid of the voices I heard at night. I cried for them as much as I cried for myself and my own life.

Yes, the White Soldier came. He came for all of us that day. One by one, we walked away from the battle with Him. The minute we had prayed for—to live—was no longer ours for which to be grateful.

There are no wars to fight now; we train for peaceful missions instead. We guard the palace and the King, for God truly is the Lord of all. We understand our purpose now in this land far away: to bring peace to a peace that already is here. We have been forgiven for the killing of the old men, young men, women, and children. Jeffery is our platoon leader now, and we drill daily. Jeffery says, "It keeps us in shape." We are preparing now for a much greater mission looming on the horizon. We will see you then, Writer. We will see you then.[16]

---

16 Perhaps Rodney was referring to Armageddon. I asked, but he just smiled instead of answering.

Duncan D.

Yes, there is much more going on than you would ever expect. This was not just a war on the ground and from the air; it was much more. The powers that be were considering dropping a nuclear weapon to end this mess. We went in to pave the way, so to speak. We didn't come out, and therefore it never happened.

Sad, isn't it, that you can't even trust your own government. We knew if we failed, there would be no record of us—who we were, where we came from, what happened to us. I've always wondered what they told our family about our deaths. Did they tell them we died honorably and were heroes? How does one go about erasing a name from our birth to our death? How can we no longer cease to exist? We are here today and gone tomorrow. Of course, only a select few knew what was coming were we to succeed. This black ops mission was well orchestrated, as they all were. We used a nuclear bomb and dropped it on Hiroshima in retaliation for Pearl Harbor. How could there be any more guilt for using it again in Vietnam?

There wasn't any way the mission could go wrong; everything had been covered again and again. It was seared into our brains—every twist and turn. Every possible obstacle we could encounter had been cussed and discussed. There was no way we could fail. But we did. When we were deep inside their perimeter, it just all exploded. They obviously knew we were coming, but how? One step lit up the whole sky. There was no way any one of us would live through that night.

And now for the good part, Writer, for we know this is what you wait for—when the White Soldier comes. So many White Soldiers came that night. Each soldier on the platoon has told you how the White Soldier came to them. It was the same for me. My White Soldier, He just stood there as if waiting for me to get my bearings. Then He saluted me and offered me His hand to help me up. I sat stunned, not fully comprehending what was happening. All around me my friends, fellow soldiers, dead. I kept asking to anyone who was listening, "What happened? What happened?" but no one answered.

"Duncan, it's time to go," He said. Kneeling down, He lifted me up, and together, with everyone else, we were just gone.

It was as if I were watching an old black and white movie in slow, very slow motion. "We failed, didn't we?" I asked Him.

"No, you didn't fail. It is as it should be. The right thing happened tonight."

At first I was stunned to hear the White Soldier say, "The right thing happened tonight." How could ten men passing ever be the "right thing?"

But God is good and patiently answered my questions. "The right thing" that happened was that the mission did not succeed, and as a result, the nuclear weapon Duncan D. spoke of was not used. Had it been, many more lives on both sides would have been lost. The devastation and loss of human life in Hiroshima and Nagasaki would have been nothing compared to that which would be destroyed in Vietnam. Not only would the Viet Cong and Vietnamese suffer, but Americans and other NATO Forces would have as well. How would our government have explained these losses to the American people?

While I had no trouble believing that within the U.S. government there had been discussion early on about using a nuclear weapon to end the war in Vietnam, it wasn't until the Pentagon Papers were declassified in July 2011 that I was able to substantiate the actual

facts.[17] In the Pentagon Papers, there are over 100 references to the possibility of using a nuclear weapon to end the war in Vietnam.

17 "The Pentagon Papers" is the nickname of a 7,000-plus-page report offiicially titled "Report of the Office of the Secretary of Defense Vietnam Task Force." Commissioned in 1967 by then secretary of defense Robert McNamera and finished in 1969, the report chronicled United States involvement in southeast Asia since World War II. Most of the report was classified as top secret. In 1971, portions of it were leaked to the press, and the *New York Times* published the first in a series of articles showing that the U.S. had been playing a role in Indochina for much longer than most of the American public knew. The articles stirred public controversy at a time when the public support for the Vietnam War was rapidly dwindling. Although the U.S. Department of Justice took legal action to stop the *New York Times* and *Washington Post* from publishing more of the report's details, the U.S. Supreme Court ruled in favor of the newspapers (*New York Times Co. v. United States*). In 2011, the full report was declassificd, and U.S. National Archives made it available to the public. Today, the Pentagon Papers can be viewed on the National Archives website, www.archives.gov/research/pentagon-papers.

Four Dog Tags

One day after I'd started to receive the spirit soldiers' stories, I clicked through eBay and found myself in the Vietnam section. How I got there I don't know; I accept that I was guided from the world of spirit.

Once there, I found an ad for dog tags—four of them. The description said they had belonged to U.S. soldiers killed in Vietnam. Not only were the name, rank, serial number, faith, and blood type readable on each tag, two of them were stained with blood.

I was horrified. From the stories the spirit soldiers had told me, I knew what many of them went through in their last minutes on earth, and to know that their bodies had then been stripped of their identification was unimaginable. To see their deaths via the world of spirit as I did was one thing; to see the actual proof of such deaths for sale on eBay was another.

I immediately bid on the dog tags with the intent to bring them home and bury them on American soil. I would try to find the families of the men they belonged to, but even if I couldn't, at least the dog tags and the spirits still connected with them would be home.[18]

I didn't pay any attention to who the seller was or where the dog tags were being sent from. Later, when I got the confirmation of my winning bid, I noticed the seller had a Vietnamese name. A week later, I received these treasures in a padded manila envelope from the seller in Da Nang.

I knew instantly these four dog tags had a role to play in this book and that the stories of the men they belonged to would be as powerful as the others I was receiving. And the synchronicity of finding these tags while I was working on this book was confirmation from the world of spirit that this book was on purpose.

When the soldiers the tags belonged to spoke with me, they thanked me for bringing them home, at least in spirit. Here are their stories.

---

18 I have been unable to locate any members of the four soldiers' families at this time, though I did attempt to do so using several different databases and a private investigator.

First Dog Tag: Johnny G.

Sweat pours off me as if it were raining. I never knew one could sweat so much. How is that? We've been pinned down here for hours; Charlie is playing a cat-and-mouse game with us tonight. It is simply a matter of who is going to make the first move. Perhaps it has evolved into a game of chess by now, as the cat found the mouse. Now it is just a matter of waiting to see which will make the first move.

My muscles ache; pins and needles shoot through my legs from the long hours of squatting. We can't kneel; it would take too long for us to stand up from a kneeling position, so we squat. At this point, I think my legs will be so numb that even if I do stand up, nothing is going to move, I will just fall face down as I try to take that first step.

There is movement somewhere down the line; I can hear it, muffled curses. That was all Charlie needed, for he had heard it too. A flare lit up the sky overhead and shots rang down on our position. Move legs—move as fast as you can. Advance forward into the black night; imagine you have the eyes of a cat and can see in the dark. What is it you see? That outline ahead. It is wrong, all wrong, out of place. Fire on it, and hope it isn't one of ours.

I look back, and the outline is gone, my chance for a kill gone. Now where is he?

A small branch cracks behind me.

Charlie doesn't take names or ask questions first; he just kills, for that is what he knows, that is what he was trained to do. There is no compassion in his killing, though I believe he does have a passion for killing. It comes so easy to him. How is that, Lord? How is it that one man can take the life of another without feeling anything?

But who am I to question killing? How many lives have I taken since that first night I set foot in-country? Did I stop to ask who it was I was killing? No, nor would I have asked had I had the time. It was live or die, and Lord, I so want to live. I did pray for them, though. Each night when I got back to my hut, I prayed for the lives I had taken that night. I prayed for any family they might have, and I prayed for my own soul, broken by each killing.

I was an intruder into a war between two cultures—Viet Cong against Vietnamese. I didn't even belong here—none of us did. We all should have been back home, working the farm, going to college, getting married, and raising our own families. This wasn't our fight, not even our war. Yet here we were trying to help the Vietnamese who could have cared less about helping themselves. Those in the villages that were outside our base were happy to just plant and harvest the rice. They answered to a different drummer, Writer. They heard the music of the ancients, and they followed that sound from the past. Their future was their past; their present was their past. So long as they followed the traditions and beliefs of their ancestors, they would be protected. This war was nothing other than a disruption to them and their way of life.

Your White Soldier came; you knew He would, didn't you, Writer? He has become a familiar figure throughout each of these stories. You were just waiting for me to tell you about His appearance. And so I shall tell you.

Charlie stood behind me, AK-47 leveled at my head. I could feel it; I didn't need to turn around see him. Yet I did want to turn around. I wanted to see him as he shot me. I slowly lowered my own weapon and raised my hands. Dawn was just beginning to break. Charlie was crazy to shoot me this close to daylight. My squad was all around me, and someone would hear the shot. Very slowly, I turned around.

It was then that I saw your White Soldier. The sun's ray had just broken the darkened sky, and there, behind Charlie, stood your White Soldier. Just as the others have described Him—spotless white mess dress with a chest full of ribbons and decorations. A feeling of calm filled that space. All of time stood still. I looked into the eyes of Charlie, and for a brief moment, I believe I saw compassion.

It was slow motion after that. Charlie fired, and someone else fired at that same instant. Charlie fell forward, I fell forward, and the White Soldier moved to stand between us. He turned slightly to salute me, and He turned back to salute Charlie. Together, we each took a hand, and like that, we were gone.

Our bodies lay out on the jungle floor just where we had left them. That sounds funny doesn't it—"where we had left them?" Yet that is just what we did: we left them.

Your White Soldier doesn't play favorites; He came for both of us that morning.

SECOND DOG TAG: ROBERT E.

Yes, in the jungles of Vietnam, life is not without its obstacles. The heat was unbearable most days. The humidity is what made it so tough on us all. I don't think anyone who came here was ready for the day-to-day weather conditions. When it wasn't hot and humid, it was wet and rainy. The dampness from the rain bothered me more than the heat, though. The rain soaked through to my bones. Back home in Seattle it was that way too. That rain would just seep through to your bones. The only difference between the Seattle rain and the Vietnam rain was the mold. After a few days of not drying out, we smelled like mold. If I could manage to get my feet dry, I was okay.

I have thought often about my choice to join the U.S. Army. Yes, it was my choice; I was not drafted, though I probably would have been down the line. I was proud to serve my country, and the thought of going to Vietnam was not a deterrent in the least. The thought process and all that goes into the pros and cons list before making such a decision is formidable. There was no one in my immediate family or circle of friends that wanted me to go. Their hope was that the war would be over before I was drafted. Most of my friends who had gone before me had not returned alive; rather, they came back in pine boxes that I helped bury in the church cemetery. There were a million reasons why I shouldn't go, and the only reason I could come up with for going was a deep welling up inside of me of pride—pride in my country, pride in my duty to serve that country. From some dark cavern deep in my soul, I knew it was my duty to serve my country. By going down and enlisting myself, I hoped to better position myself within the army machine.

I thought long and hard about the killing aspect. I questioned myself and my faith, asking myself over and over, "Could I kill another human being? Was I capable of such an act?" I wrestled with this question day and night before I finally found a peace somewhere in between yes and no. I knew I had to trust God to know when it was right or wrong to take another's life. I can say now, He didn't let me down. Even in the midst of a firestorm of bullets, I waited for His guidance.

Some of you may be saying that I obviously waited too long to react one too many times since I too came back in a pine box, but that is not the case. I listened to God, and I did not fire when I had the chance. You see, for me, this war was a test of my faith and my obedience to God, not about a war on foreign soil. There was a reason that God spared the young Vietnamese boy that stood before me, holding a weapon far too heavy and large for his small stature. He was an easy target, and for sure my experience would have beaten him to the trigger. But I heard God's voice telling me to not shoot, and I didn't. The young boy and I stared at each other, our eyes looking deep into each other's soul. What was it we would see within the other? Did either of us really want to be in the position we were in? He was far too young to know about war and the atrocities it brought. Who had trained this young man? Who were his parents? Would they be proud to know he was out on a battlefield instead of at home learning in school?

I looked away, just for a moment, to see a flash of bright light beside me. In that light stood your White Soldier, Writer. I don't remember feeling the bullet penetrate my heart. I guess my looking away gave the young shooter permission to kill me. Or perhaps he took the opportunity because I looked away, and he couldn't kill me while our eyes held out hope that there might be another way to end this bloody war. It was as the others have all said: quick, painless, and dignified. I came into this war with God in my heart; I left with Him walking beside me, holding me up as I leaned on Him for support. Can't think of a better way to go, Writer. Can you?

I hope that young Vietnamese boy who became a man that day grew up into a different man, one that abhorred killing and turned to a peaceful way of life. I hope there was a silent exchange between our souls of love for one another as another human being, one not bound by race, color, or creed. I could only pray that I was his first and last kill. Knowing that, I would feel my life had counted and I had, in the end, made a difference in a country not my own. I was proud to serve my country. In serving my country, I had also served my God. I did not fail either—or myself.

THIRD DOG TAG: JIM D.

Jim was part of the patrol whose stories are told in "A Covert Mission" earlier in this chapter. Like the soldiers in that patrol, he died on June 15, 1971. I have chosen to separate his story from theirs because of its relevance to this section.

My leaving was quicker than most. We had just choppered in and were hovering above the ground. "Jump," was all I heard before I felt the sting of a bullet penetrate my helmet. I tumbled forward, and the chopper began a quick ascent as more shots rang out. What the f_ _k? I wanted to scream, but nothing came from my lips.

He stood there tall and proud, your White Soldier. That's what you are after, isn't it? My story? I looked up at him through a sea of red blood. Damn the luck, I had just barely made it in-country, and this happens.

"I'm not going to make it out of this one, am I?" I asked Him.

"No, son, not this one, not this time."

"Damn the bad luck." I knew something was going to happen. I had felt it early on; my stomach churned, and my gut told me to duck, but I hadn't listened.

"Shall we go?" He said, as He saluted me before picking me up. He carried me off that landing zone and into the brush, and then we were just *gone.*

I know this isn't much of a story and pretty short, but it is what it is. That's the story you are after, the one about the White Soldier. The rest is not important. In case no one thinks to thank you for bringing us home and burying us on America's soil, thank you.

Our bodies didn't make it home, and you know why; just leave it at that. The time has passed in which to bring out our mission. Just let it go. There is no need to follow that thread any further. Sometimes it is best to let sleeping dogs lie, especially this time. Your mind is already churning up research techniques you could employ to sniff out if what we have said is true. Let it lie and leave it alone. It was a long time ago in a country not our own. So many lives were changed just at the thought of annihilation of another. We [the United States] did it in Hiroshima; we should have learned the lesson then. We did it first and now rail at the thought of another country developing their nuclear weapons program. How dare them! Yet we had no problem thinking about doing it again. What does that say about us as a society? We never would have been able to get our men out fast enough, and so many would have been lost at our own hand. How could we, as a nation, ever think that it was right to do it again?

Fourth Dog Tag: Tommy K.

Look hard and try to find my parents, please, Writer. It is important to them to have a small remembrance of me.[19] In some way, it will let them find peace and allow me to rest in peace in return. You can do it—find them for me. You are guided; allow the White Soldier to guide you to them.

Now you want my story, I suppose? Well, for what it is worth, here it is. I had been in the country far too long by my account. One year was my tour of duty; that's what my orders said. Somehow or other, that date kept getting pushed back. There was a lot going on in the unit, and no one seemed to have time to find out why I wasn't on a bird [helicopter] out of here. There was a hush over the camp, lots of individuals speaking softly in groups of one or two, but never more. Being a grunt [a low-ranking soldier], I wasn't privy to all the hushed communications, but I knew. I knew it was something big; it had to be for all that was going on at this time.

Even my buddies were acting different. It was as if everyone that had been chosen was in some way making preparations just in case they didn't come back. Letters were being written home like crazy; material possessions were being given away. Those of us that didn't seem to be in on the inner circle of secrecy were given souvenirs with instructions to

19 I have not been able to find his parents as of yet.

make sure they got to a certain person if the soldier didn't make it back. I guess I felt jealous that I hadn't been included this time. I had gone on all the other top-secret missions. Why not this one?

A new camaraderie was forming amongst the group of ten who had been picked. They ate together, slept together, gathered together for briefing sessions throughout the days that led up to the June fifteenth event.[20] My best friend, Johnny—I call him Johnny [Jeremiah S.]—was part of the group. You already have his story. He looked at me differently now, I wasn't one of "them." It was like I had become the enemy. I tried to speak with him when I saw him off on his own, but he turned away from me. Oh, how that hurt. We had been through so much together. Perhaps in his own way he was just trying to spare me from the hurt if he didn't make it back. All I could think to say was, "Stay safe and keep your head down, man." You know, those were my last words to him. They left undercover of the dark that night. I never saw him again.

In fact, once everyone had left, my orders came down. I was going home. I had my stuff all gathered up and sat, ready to go, when the chopper landed. As sun broke over the mountains to the east, I heard the *thuwack-thuwack-thuwack* of the blades in the distance. There were three of us leaving that day,

---

20 Tommy is referring to the patrol went out on the covert mission described earlier in this chapter, but never returned from it.

two officers and myself. Putting a grunt with the brass [officers]—who would have seen that coming? We all headed to the landing zone, ducking low to keep from getting hit with the chopper blast as it settled to the ground. We were waved off as the pilot jumped out and ran to the colonel's tent. A few seconds later, the two officers I was with were called into the tent. A pall seemed to take over the camp as everyone stopped what they were doing to listen to the hushed tones coming from inside.

There had been an incident with the team that had left last night. All had been lost. The pilot with the two officers left the colonel's tent. He waved at me to follow him to the chopper. Climbing aboard, we strapped ourselves into the jump seat. I could tell that whatever had happened had been terrible news. The officers both looked off in opposite directions. I could see tears streaming from their eyes.

"My friend Johnny went out with the team last night," I said staring at my hands folded in my lap. "He's not coming back, is he?" I asked looking from one officer to the other.

"No, soldier, he's not," said the officer closest to me. "Something went terribly wrong last night, terribly wrong."

I too looked off to the east to watch the sun rise further in the sky. Tears for my friend Johnny and the other men that had passed that night slid down my face. I wasn't ashamed to cry. Sometimes it is okay to cry. This was one of those times.

We were to have a few days off in Saigon for out-processing before we headed home. All of a sudden, heading home didn't sound like the right thing to do. I had to find out what happened to Johnny. All I could think of was that I had to go back. I headed back to the unit out-processing and told the first shirt that I wanted to go back to my unit to find out about my buddy. Unfortunately, that wasn't going to happen, and he told me to go back to my barracks and wait for my flight out of 'Nam, as I had been in-country far too long.

I was so angry—angry at myself, angry at Johnny, angry at all the people along the way that wouldn't let me go back. I hit the local bar and drowned my sorrow in the local beer served by the all-too-accommodating local girls. I was so wasted by the time the bar fight started, I don't even know who started it, but by God, I was going to finish it. I finished it; it finished me. Shots rang out and seemed to just spray us all as if, water coming out of a hose. So many lives lost that night. Why?

Yes, I feel your anticipation. You can't wait to know about your White Soldier and how He came to gather us all up. There was blood everywhere. The local girls were screaming. The local security forces were yelling for everyone to get down on the floor. Those that weren't already dead lay down amongst the dead. That's all I remember before I and several others stood up out of our bodies to follow the White Soldier. He saluted us, just like everyone says, and gathered us up and off we marched. We were going home.

You know I saw Johnny again. He was waiting for me when we arrived. It was as if yesterday had never happened, as if he hadn't left in the middle of the night and I hadn't left at sunrise. We are together again, Writer, together again.

The Greatest Sacrifice

As I came to the end of the soldiers' stories in "A Covert Mission," I found myself curious about what had really happened to the small group of soldiers who had all passed on June 15 of the same year. I decided to see if their names were on the Vietnam Veterans Memorial in Washington, DC. When I couldn't find them on "the Wall," I called a friend who is a private investigator for help.[21] *He was able to provide me with enough information to know that the U.S. government had participated in a cover-up involving these soldiers. The social security numbers of the men in "Four Dog Tags" were legitimately assigned to the named soldiers, but the military records were*

---

21 It has been estimated that the Vietnam Veterans Memorial is missing the names of over 6,000 veterans who served in Vietnam. In July 2012, a Vietnam veterans activists group forced over 550,000 "lost" service records to be made public. Many of those records belonged to servicemen who participated in top-secret military operations during the Vietnam War. Perhaps now the names uncovered will be added to the memorial where they belong, with the names of the war's other heroes. ("Vietnam Veterans" Yahoo list. message from Gary, subject: "Ghost Walkers, Missing Records," July 29, 2012.)

missing for all four. Further research showed that not all official military lists accurately contain the names of military members.

The men on the mission had been erased for all intents and purposes. They knew going in that if they did not succeed they would no longer exist. Not even their families would know their fate; their families would be told only, "They did not return."

When I asked the men, "What is up with none of your names being on the Vietnam wall? Were you involved in a black ops mission?" Jeffery C. came forward to answer.

I think you already know, Writer. There is no need to write the question. You already know the answer. We are the forgotten—left behind and forgotten. There was so much going on in those last years in-country that it is no wonder we were forgotten.

There is a political side to all of this, yes, and a cover-up too, but that is not why we are telling our stories. We are telling our stories so we are not forgotten, ever. Your mission is to just bring forth our words and hear us now. We are "real," are we not? Do you not see us as we speak? Have you not traveled with us deep into the jungles to capture our stories of our last minutes on the earth plane? Did you not feel our pain and wipe the blood from our mouths as we said goodbye one last time? You were there as an observer, writing our stories, but you were with us nonetheless.

Let go of chasing the cover-up; someone else will pick it up and run with it. Stay with us and write, Writer. Write our stories for others to hear and experience, for you certainly have a ringside seat.

Our names should be on the wall along with all our other fallen comrades, but we understand why they are not. It had to be this way. We knew the consequences going in. We were told beforehand we would be forgotten, erased actually, if we didn't succeed. Now you, too, know the outcome of this mission we undertook. Our families didn't forget us, though. They will always remember us, for we were their children, and some of us still babes, wet behind the ears, if the truth be told. But we were brave—yes, we were, Writer. It isn't so bad not having our names on the wall. For we live on in the minds of our brothers who returned home. They have carried our secret for far too long. It is time to let it go.

Now it is time to move forward, leave the past behind and move into the future. It is because of the past that you have a future, and we are proud to have given you that future, to have been a part of giving that future to each of you. It was our duty, it was our honor, and it was our last great sacrifice in this lifetime. What is life, anyway, if it is not lived knowing that the greatest gift is giving one's life in exchange for another life? Nothing else really matters, does it?

4

Returning Home

Now I wear my Vietnam Veteran ball cap, and
people say "Welcome home."
George, Ton San Nhut, 1970–1971

When Timothy, the veteran who shared the story of his arrival in Vietnam in chapter 1, returned from the war, he brought a healing message to other veterans. When he first came to me through the world of spirit, he was still alive on the physical plane. But when he returned to tell me this story of his homecoming, he had passed, and his spirit had returned home to world of spirit.

So many men gave their life for that war. So many young men never got to live out the dreams of their youth. And for what was their sacrifice? They were intruders in a land that didn't want them there, and those that did survive returned to a country that hated, despised them even more for their role in the horror that unfolded in Vietnam.

Instead of a hero's welcome home, they received a cold shoulder, angry and hateful names hurled at them. They were ostracized from those who they needed most to understand, those they needed to feel safe sharing their stories of horror and unspeakable events with. Who was there to welcome them home? Who was there to listen to their stories?

The horrors of war played out on your television set and in your papers. At any time did you stop and put yourself in the boots of the soldier acting on orders to commit atrocities far beyond his capability? You could beat the draft if you had a family name and money; only then did the rules not apply.

In order to survive my tour in Vietnam, I had to put my life in perspective. I had to remember not to dwell on day-to-day events, but to think ahead till the day I would leave and return to the farm and my family. When I did get home at the end of my tour, I was not greeted with a hero's welcome. Only my family met me at the bus station. What had happened to our small farming community? How had it changed while I was gone? Why had it changed?

My pop was no scholar. In fact, he hadn't finished the eighth grade in his time. But my pop was smart, the common-sense kind of smart. We spent quite a few evenings out under the old oak tree by the pond after chores were done, talking about what I had experienced. I felt guilty for having to kill another human being. I wanted him to know how much it hurt me to do so, as I had been raised not to kill. I wanted him to know that it wasn't his fault; he had taught me well. I did what I had to do to survive, and I had survived. So many of my friends did not make it home.

When I felt better about myself, I went and shared with my pastor. Pastor Jack approached it from a different light. He talked about grieving and what he had learned from his years of being a pastor and praying with people and comforting them when loved ones died or were dying. In many ways, I, too, had died. The Timothy that left the farm was not the same Timothy that came home. Sometime during that year away, I had died and been reborn. Death and dying teach such great life lessons. Who would have known?

Pastor Jack told me the first stage of grief is denial.[22] In the weeks before my leaving, denial had run through every conversation I had, both silent and out loud. I couldn't believe it was, in fact, happening to me—the draft, that is. I was just an Iowa farm boy. I had roots in the deep, rich earth of

---

22 The Elisabeth Kübler-Ross Foundation, "Five Stages of Grief," article online. Available at www.ekrfoundation.org/five-stages-of-grief.

my family's farm. How would I carry on my family lineage as a farmer? Why me, Lord? Why me?

The second stage is anger. How angry can one person become? What are the consequences of that anger? I had hated every minute I was alive from the day I received my draft notice. I knew nothing of Vietnam, only stories I had heard from friends who returned and the families of those who didn't. You can bet I was angry. Much of that anger, although not directed at my family, fell upon their shoulders anyway. War didn't happen to good people. I wanted to hold onto something to believe in. I was a good person. Why was it happening to me?

The third stage, Pastor Jack told me, is bargaining. What did I have worthy enough to trade my life for? I didn't have much, nothing monetary and certainly nothing of material value. Laughingly, I told God I would give up my sister if I had one. I'm sure He had no use for the old dog that wandered the farm.

The fourth stage is depression. I had fallen into deep depression thinking about my failure as a man, as I saw it anyways. I obviously wasn't lucky, as my number had come up for the draft. I had nothing of value to bargain for. What had I done wrong? Why me? I felt sadness that I had let Mom and Dad down and fear of the unknown that awaited me on the other side of that bus ride that was to come all too quickly.

Finally, when there is nothing left, there is acceptance. I accepted that I had been chosen to go and fight for my country. Perhaps I had been chosen to go so I could return and help others to heal.

Pastor Jack took my hands and turned them over, palms up. Barely visible now, scars, once callouses, remained from all the [farm] work I had done over the years. My hands were smoother now. Perhaps being wet all the time [in Vietnam] had softened my hands.

"These are still the hands of that Iowa farm boy that left a year ago, full of fear and a sense of failure. What was it I told you before you left, son?" Pastor Jack asked me.

"You quoted to me from Isaiah," I said. "'They that wait upon the Lord shall renew their strength; they shall mount up with wings like eagles; they shall run and not be weary, they shall walk and not faint.'"[23]

"You remembered," he said, smiling. "You were always my best student. You came through on the wings of the eagle, Tim. You did what you had to do. I know you aren't proud of the killing part. How could anyone be proud of that? You did what you had to do to survive, and you are alive to tell about your experiences. Share with others, Tim. Accept what has been given you. Share with others what it was like for you in the jungles, always on alert at every sound you heard, every movement you saw out of the corner of your eye. Share about the men who fell

23 Isaiah 40:31, *The Living Bible*

at your side, the horrors you saw and experienced. This is your story, Tim, the story you were meant to tell."

I did go on and tell my story, Writer, to anyone who would listen. I began that Sunday in church. Pastor Jack said he was happy to get a break from preaching the sermon for a couple of weeks. I was scared at first, even more frightened than that first night in the jungle, where I knew the worst thing that could happen to me was death. There, in the pulpit, in front of all those people, most of them family and friends, I was at a loss as to how they would receive my story. But if I could change one heart by opening up a window for someone to see the war as I saw it through my eyes, then perhaps the next soldier coming home will have a hero's welcome like they deserve. And so I began:

> Once upon a time in the land of dragons and fairies, into the verdant green jungles of a place far from home, a soldier came—many soldiers. Young men, some still considered young boys by their mothers, were dropped through the jungle canopy to emerge in a war zone below. The canopy of green was deceiving. From ten thousand feet in the air, it resembled heads of broccoli. It was lighter in color perhaps, but still crowns of the trees bunched together. Underneath the canopy, were jungles of death and destruction. I was but one of those young men, just eighteen at the time I was drafted. . . .

5

A Synchronicity of Events

Synchronicity is the experience of two or more events that are apparently causally unrelated or unlikely to occur together by chance, yet are experienced as occurring together in a meaningful manner.

"Synchronicity," entry in Wikipedia

WRESTLING WITH THE VIETNAM WAR

At first, I didn't feel qualified to write this book about the Vietnam War and its soldiers, because I had not served in Vietnam. But once I began writing this book, I began to see how events from my past had, in fact, paved the way for me to relive my own memories of those Vietnam War years. In doing so, I needed to reconcile my feelings about the war and my own military service during those years. Exposing my thoughts and memories to light brought up some interesting discoveries and healing.

When I was in high school, I had written letters to soldiers in Vietnam, as well as read obituaries, until I graduated and went away to college. I told myself I was giving up on both writing letters and noticing the local newspaper's obituary column because of my need to focus on my studies. Perhaps that was just an excuse to get away from my feelings about the war and the toll it was taking on my friends.

Six years later, I enlisted in the U.S. Army to serve my country, believing it was the patriotic thing to do. Looking back now with new eyes, a new wisdom, I see that by enlisting, I was doing something to assuage my guilt over not being there for my friends, for those who were serving, and for those who had died.

I served as a Specialist 5 in the U.S. Army during what is considered the Vietnam Era (August 8, 1964 to May 7, 1975). At the time I volunteered, the U.S. Army regulations mandated by Congress restricted women from combat assignments. Women were allowed to work in support positions in combat zones, but could not be assigned a combat military occupational specialty (MOS). I served with the Tenth Special Forces at Fort Devens, Massachusetts (thirty miles west of Boston), and later in the Panama Canal Zone at the School of the Americas.

As a member of the armed forces, I was a soldier trained to kill, and I was willing to give my life for my country's freedom should the need arise. Like many of the soldiers I, too, wrote my last letter home.

In 1986, I found the book of poetry called *Johnny's Song: Poetry of a Vietnam Veteran* by Steven Mason.[24] My feelings of guilt increased as I read what soldiers returning from Vietnam had experienced and what they were continuing to experience. I knew how hurtful it was to feel unwelcomed, to not receive a thank you for their service upon returning home to American soil. I began to purposely search out soldiers and veterans to say thank you for their service.

Also at that time, I was working as a paralegal for a Las Vegas attorney named Marshal Willick, who wrote *Military Retirement Benefits in Divorce: A Lawyer's Guide to Valuation and Distribution*, the first textbook in this subject area, for the American

---

24 Steven Mason, *Johnny's Song: Poetry of a Vietnam Veteran* (New York: Bantam Books, 1986).

Bar Association in 1998. His work with military members encouraged me to entertain the idea of becoming an attorney to fight for the rights of all veterans. At the time, I made a series of choices that took me down a different path. Still, I did what I could for the veterans and active-duty military families in my position as wife of a U.S. Air Force commander.

When my husband retired from the U.S. Air Force after twenty-seven years, my path again took me away from the military world. It would only be on the streets and in airports that I had the opportunity to thank soldiers, both men and women, for their service. I began to expand my gratitude beyond just a thank you. When I see a soldier [in uniform] in line at a coffee or fast food place, I buy their coffee or meal. In restaurants I thank them for their service and pick up their tab. I do my best to be inconspicuous when doing so.

It wasn't until Jeffery C. came through the sea of children in 2011 that I realized what else I could do to help veterans, specifically Vietnam veterans. I could listen to their stories and write them down for others to share.

It was at about that time that I happened into eBay and found the dog tags of four American soldiers being sold by someone in Vietnam (see "Four Dog Tags" in chapter 3). The suppressed anger I'd been holding about the war and our country for its involvement in Vietnam exploded. I was bound and determined to give voice to everyone who wanted to come forward with their stories. I purchased the dog tags. The soldiers they'd belonged to had picked me to listen to them, and listen to them I did.

These four dog tags will be interred in hallowed ground at the Museum of Forgotten Warriors.[25]

25 Museum of Forgotten Warriors, 5865 "A" Road, Marysville, CA 95901

My Own Journey to Vietnam

In an effort to understand the energy and spirit of the land, I traveled to Vietnam in April, 2012. I visited Ho Chi Minh City, formerly known as Saigon; the Mekong Delta Region, the rice basket of South Vietnam; and Nha Trang, one of several coastal resort towns frequented by soldiers on R&R during the war years.

At the time of my trip, Timothy, the narrator whose story appears in chapter 1 and who recounts his homecoming in chapter 4, had passed from the earth plane and was now in the world of spirit. He served as my consummate travel guide, having offered me the challenge of seeing Vietnam through his eyes early on in our conversations. We met up in spirit upon my arrival in Phu My.

Every so often, I saw above-ground tombs rising in the corner of the local rice paddies. I wondered how many of our young men might be buried in those same fields. Off record, I was told that the Vietnamese people had buried our fallen soldiers out of respect. Those same soldiers still needed to be accounted for by the U.S. government so that their families would have closure. These soldiers are officially considered missing in action (MIA), lost as they are in the shadow world of rural Vietnamese burials. While the U.S. military cannot account for all its soldiers, American servicemen are still there, resting in peace where they fell. A total of 980

Americans missing from the Vietnam War have been identified since 1973, including 687 in Vietnam and the others in Laos and Cambodia, according to the Joint POW/MIA Accounting Command (JPAC).[26] There are still 1,666 Americans unaccounted for from the war, including 1,284 in Vietnam.[27]

We went from Phu My to Saigon to the Mekong Delta and back. Timothy, being familiar with the area we were in, pointed out several graves as I traveled through it.

"My buddy Dan died in that field. See it there? Right there in the corner." Timothy nudged my shoulder and pointed out the van window. "So many of our men are still buried in those rice paddies. So many."

I wanted to ask Timothy if Dan was still among the missing, but I didn't.

Nearing the site of the former U.S. embassy, the last place of American presence before the fall of Saigon (April 29, 1975), I saw the caved-in roof over one section of the building. The embassy has

---

26 The U.S. Joint POW/MIA Accounting Command conducts global search, recovery, and laboratory operations to identify unaccounted-for Americans from past conflicts in order to support the Department of Defense's personnel accounting efforts. See the command's website at www.jpac.pacom.mil, for more details.

27 David Alexander, "Vietnam Opens Three Restricted Sites for U.S. MIA Hunt," *Chicago Tribune* (June 4, 2012). Available at www.chicagotribune.com/news/sns-rt-us-vietnam-usa-miabre8530be-20120604,0,374753.story.

been repurposed and is in use today as the U.S. consulate, and the damaged section is closed up from the inside of the building.

Timothy told me, “But for the bullet shells in the walls and the missing roofs, the inner city of Saigon looks today as it did before the war.”

Most likely, the same families are still sitting in the same doorways, selling the same products as they did before the war. The outer landscape may change, but the inner circle never does. In the center of the hustle and bustle of this city of five million people, there is simplicity of living. The common Vietnamese live each day in the present moment. Tomorrow will come, and when it does, they will get through it just as they have always done.

Leaving Saigon, we drove alongside the Mekong Delta River, now black with sludge from human waste, garbage, and years of neglect. Across the river new tri-level houses dotted the landscape, set amongst the decaying buildings of the past.

Later, we traveled down a tributary of the Mekong Delta by sampan, a relatively flat-bottomed boat made out of bamboo and capable of navigating in only a few inches of water. Our sampan could travel unseen under the dense overhanging vegetation lining the banks of the many rivers and tributaries along the Mekong Delta.

I could only imagine what our soldiers must have gone through as they entered this same tributary back in the war. They truly were sitting ducks for the Viet Cong snipers. Jungle rises up on both sides of the river, and light shows through only in places where the forest canopy allows it to. Occasionally another tributary will fork off, supposedly to meet up with other waterways.

As exciting as this ride was for me, because I had never been on a sampan or the Mekong Delta before, I felt Timothy stiffen as he sat down beside me. During the war, his company had been called the River Rats and spent their time patrolling deep into the tributaries and waterways.

We were fed an elephant ear fish from the river, deep-fried, whole. As it stood propped up on a board to drain, its scales lifted up and fell off as it cooled. I was leery of eating the meat, considering it had come from the dirty, muddy river, but Timothy egged me on. So I ate a piece of the sweetest white meat and cucumber wrapped in rice paper that I have ever tasted. I found that if you bless whatever it is you eat, you won't get sick. I did a lot of food blessing in Vietnam.

Spring rolls were made of some type of meat (I didn't ask) wrapped in a crunchy noodle nest. Tamarind sauce with very hot chilies added is the dip of choice. Slices of pineapple were served with the traditional sea salt and chili-powder topping. How salt cuts the sour and turns pineapple sweet I don't know. I do know that I won't eat pineapple again without sea salt and chilies. Other dishes were eagerly enjoyed by us all.

All the while we ate, Timothy stood at my shoulder, telling me of his own experience with these same foods.

"Puke—all I did was puke, day and night, until my gut finally accepted the foul odor and tastes. We ate all their same foods so we would smell like them. That is important out here, smell. It is so heightened, a survival mechanism."

While I was only in Vietnam a few days and saw only a small portion of her land, I felt contentment from the people I met, even those in poverty. The war of forty years ago was nothing other than an annoyance to them. The land owned her people; they did not own her.

Timothy was quiet for most of my travels while in Vietnam, only speaking to point out sights of interest familiar to him. His quietness allowed me the opportunity to see, hear, and experience Vietnam on my own time. Late into the night, he and I would talk about the places we had visited. Like Timothy, I too fell in love with the beauty and spirit of place.

The Land Speaks

I channeled the following two poems as I held a vial of water from the Mekong Delta and a vial of sand from Nha Trang beach. The spirits of both the water and sand came through the world of spirit much like the voices of people do. I have chosen to include them because they speak of our servicemen during their time in Vietnam.

Voice of the Mekong Delta

I am the lifeblood of this country,
My water flows through her pulsating veins.

Without my life, she would die.
She would dry up and blow away.

Her skin would crack and through the crack
All would hear the cries of the ancestors.

Angry their children had not taken care of her
The land to which they had given
birth, the land they loved.

For it is my spirit that lives in
the heart of these people,
My spirit moves them forward each day.

Though my waters have been soiled by war,
Dirtied by the spoilage of living,
Still I run, giving sustenance to
my people and yours.

I am the lifeblood of this country,
As my water flows through her pulsating veins.

Voice of Nha Trang Sand

I am the sand of memories past and present,
Your young men frolicked on my beaches,
Crying tears for the horrors they had seen.

Digging holes in my bosom they buried memories
of time spent in our jungles.
Still, they built sand castles, hoping for a future,
a fortress of protection and strength.

Their tears did not stay in my bosom long,
Tides came and washed them out to sea
Sad memories don't belong here.

All that remain are memories of happy times,
times they left the jungle behind.
Finding pleasure with another
lost and hurting soul
nestled in my arms.

My shores crawled with hurting souls,
souls displaced from their homes and families.
For that is what war does,
it displaces hearts and souls.

6

A Gathering of Heroes

A veteran is someone who, at one point in his life wrote a blank check made payable to "The United States of America" for an amount "up to and including his/her life."
Anonymous

After writing this book and honoring the voices and their stories, I believed I was finished for the moment. Instead, one night when I could not sleep, I arose, listened, and went to my keyboard. The soldiers had gathered together once more to come through from the world of spirit and collectively share their wisdom.

We have wars so we can continue to evolve and learn to find forgiveness. The only reason for killing is so that those living can experience finding forgiveness for the one who has killed. Remember, the physical body dies and passes into decay, but the soul is up and away, back in heaven. There is a physical death, but not a spiritual death, for the soul lives on to experience another lifetime, if it chooses.

Until there is total peace, there will always be wars and other challenges presented. Wars test the metal from which we are created. War affords a young man or woman the opportunity to discover the very best in themselves—an opportunity to step up and make a difference in another's life.

So long as there is fear, greed, anger, and hatred amongst you, there will be wars. When the lion lays down with the lamb, when the two can coexist together without fear between them, then and only then will there be peace. Peace comes from within, not from without. Peace isn't something you can buy off a shelf, nor can you bargain for it. True peace is achieved when one lets go of all fear, greed, anger, and hatred for another who has taken the life of a loved one.

Killing, be it in a war, at a school, at a theater, down the block, or around the corner, is an event that affords many souls the opportunity to grow and evolve away from the killing fields. Fathers, mothers, brothers, sisters, and other relatives; friends and communities; even nations—all are presented with an opportunity to find compassion and forgiveness. Forgiving our enemies is an ancient message of growth and healing.

Long before each soul involved came into this lifetime, it agreed beforehand to meet and be part of the killing act. Killings are not random acts of violence against others. They are carefully orchestrated by each soul involved. There are no random acts of violence. They may appear that way to you, but they are not.

Our soul groups work together with each other through all the many different lifetimes. Sometimes we will be the killer, sometimes the one who is killed. Whatever the circumstances, we are working together with the others to evolve our souls.

Killing has never been something that comes naturally to any soul, not even those throughout history who have appeared to have found it easy to kill. All the soldiers have come to show how far we have to go to find forgiveness—not just a pronouncement of forgiveness, but heartfelt forgiveness that is apparent through actions. You cannot be the lamb or lay down with the lion until you have truly forgiven one another and that forgiveness runs through your soul. Only then will you not be eaten, and there will be peace between you.

You have told our stories well, Writer, and we thank you for your gift of communication. You are correct. There are so many more stories to tell.

At the end of their message, a hush fell over the crowd of soldiers. As they snapped to attention, a pilot walked down the aisle that opened among them. I knew he was a pilot by the flight suit he wore, the instrument board strapped to his leg, his helmet and air mask. I knew he was a pilot because he was my father, and with him walked the White Soldier.

"No one passes alone," my father said. "No one passes alone."

I sought to linger in spirit with the soldiers, my father, and God, because when I was with them, for once I felt total peace. Still, I knew it was time to leave and return my spirit to the physical plane. Coming to attention, I said, "Thank you for your service" to the soldiers and all who stood before me. I raised my right hand in salute one last time.

I know from my own experience with the passing of my father that until fear and hurt is exposed to the light, no healing can occur, and one stays locked behind the wall of their own making. I am grateful for the soldiers who came through to share their stories and open their wounds to the light. Through their stories, I have found solace and healing in the knowledge that the White Soldier was also there with my father at the time of his passing. I no longer fear my own passing or think I will be alone when that time comes. I know the White Soldier will come for me as He did for each of those who have gone before, and He will continue to come so long as there is war.

Epilogue

I saw Timothy the other day, sitting on a bench underneath the bridge in what was formerly a local park, a resting place frequented by veterans of several wars. I heard him begin his sermon:

> Once upon a time in the land of dragons and fairies, into the verdant green jungles of a place far from home, a soldier came—many soldiers. Young men, some still considered young boys by their mothers, were dropped through the jungle canopy to emerge in a war zone below. The canopy of green was deceiving. From ten thousand feet in the air, it resembled heads of broccoli. It was lighter in color perhaps, but still the crowns of the trees bunched together. Underneath the canopy, were jungles of death and destruction. I was but one of those young men, just eighteen at the time I was drafted. . . .

My vision blurred as tears gathered in my eyes. The spirit soldier next to him was in battle uniform, an M-16 resting across his lap. Head bowed and hands held as if he were praying, he was lost somewhere in the fog of battle. Timothy leaned over and whispered in his ear, loud enough for all in the world of spirit and myself to hear, "Thank you for your service, sir. Thank you for your service."

If you would like to assist a veteran and thank them for their military service, there are ways to help. Some days you may see a veteran sitting in the park or standing on a street corner with a cardboard sign asking for food. Almost every restaurant has a gift certificate for a meal or two; hand that veteran one and take a moment to tell him, "Thank you for your service."

Perhaps you have time to spend in a veterans' hospital reading to veterans whose life's journey is slowly coming to an end or listening as they share their thoughts and stories. If you have a Department of Veterans Affairs in your town, I'm sure they welcome volunteers for whatever time you might be able to share.

Research veteran organizations; there are thousands of them out there. If you can't spare your time, donations are always welcome. I am familiar with two such organizations: Soldiers Heart (www.soldiersheart.net) and Wounded Warriors Project (www.woundedwarriorproject.org).

If you are ever near Marysville, California, take the extra time to stop by the Museum of Forgotten

Warriors (www.museumoftheforgottenwarrior.org), a moving and inspirational place that honors and remembers our soldiers of all wars.

Whatever you can do to show a veteran you care will be appreciated and well remembered. As Timothy shared his story in churches across America's farmlands, he learned that a kind word goes miles to mend the hurts of yesterday.

Afterword
A Message of My Own

I came into this lifetime to learn lessons for my soul's growth and evolution—perhaps to relearn lessons my soul had forgotten or lessons not truly learned in previous lifetimes. Without lessons, our lives stagnate, and our souls do not grow. We do not evolve, and we go nowhere.

Being a communicator has taken me on quite a journey. Speaking with the world of spirit is something I do for my own pleasure. Cancer helped me to see that being a communicator is who I am and what I do. It is my pleasure to bring forth these stories from the soldiers.

Thanks to the New Age movement, doors have opened for people such as me, who communicate with the world of spirit, to come out and be accepted in public. I was no longer shunned for what I did. At first, people searched me out to communicate with the spirits of their pets who had passed. Of those, many didn't believe I could talk with the spirit of their Aunt Suzy or Uncle Jim, nor did they believe that they themselves could communicate with their loved ones.

Knowing I still have access to those who have passed from my life gives me hope that while physical death of the body is permanent, the soul and spirit live on, and the souls and spirits of our loved ones who have passed are only a thought away. I now celebrate a passing, rather than grieve. I am sad to see whomever it is go, but I know they live on in a much better place, and I will be reunited with them when my own time to pass comes.

There is no doubt in my mind that on the day I cross over, there will be a huge crowd gathered and waiting for me. I know there will be a room full of angels and spirits in various shapes, sizes, and forms to take me across the rainbow bridge. I even expect to see the White Soldier coming for me as He came for all these soldiers and my father.

I end this book knowing that I am a good person and that my gift of communication is just that—a gift. I am blessed to be able to speak to two worlds, the seen and unseen, and I am never alone. Nor are you.

Spirits clamber at the door of my mind so I can write their stories. I understand my life's purpose is to open that door and let them in. What you have just finished reading is another of God's seventh-wave answers to the question of my life's purpose. This is the second set of stories from the world of spirit coming through to speak. I am a communicator, and I am proud to be their writer.

I am gifted by God, and so are you. In your quiet space, just ask yourself, "What if this truly is possible?" Then listen for God's answer. May your own journey be as blessed as mine has been.

Acknowledgments

When I wrote *When Spirits Speak: Messages from Spirit Children* (2011), I believed it took a village of many people to produce a book. Now, a year later, I realize it still takes a village, but my village has grown and changed. This time, my teachers have been those I questioned about the land known as Vietnam and who shared their experiences with me.

Perhaps it was the subject matter of this book—the Vietnam War—that caused the change in village members and brought me new voices, new friends, and new ideas.

As I wrote, I realized that whatever one's position on the Vietnam War, it is important to reach out to the soldiers who have come forth with their stories—those who have passed, as well as those soldiers still living today. May those servicemen and -women who have given the ultimate sacrifice always be remembered. To their families who miss them the most, especially the sons and daughters of those servicemen and -women, thank you for your own sacrifice each and every day. We are free to live in America because of our military members' unselfish service to our country.

To the many soldiers and Vietnam veterans who came home, but have since passed, and who shared their lives and stories with me, my sincere, eternal gratitude.

To my dad, who served his country in World War II and who gave his life during his U.S. Navy service, and to my mom who always supported him, my thanks for instilling in me my own patriotic duty.

To my husband Kurt whose own military service of 27 years has allowed me the opportunity to experience military life as a military spouse and spend my days writing the stories those from the world of spirit wish to share.

To my daughter, Teri Ann "Sunny" Henderson whose illustration "Last Letter Home" graces this book. You are so talented and gifted in your own right.

To all those who assisted in the publication process of this book, my editors Amy Rost and Pamela Johnson, my Balboa Press Design Team and friends who helped further my research, your assistance was invaluable.

To the sea, my forever friend, thank you for the seventh wave once again, source of solace and creativity.